BRITISH OLYMPIC HEROES

The Best of British Gold Medallists

Kitty Carruthers

British Olympic Heroes
The Best of British Gold Medallists

Medina Publishing Ltd
83 Ewell Road
Surbiton
Surrey KT6 6AH
United Kingdom

© Medina Publishing 2012

ISBN: 978-0-9567081-1-3

CIP Data: A catalogue record for this book is
available from the British Library

Designed by Kitty Carruthers
Printed and bound by Short Run Press, Exeter

Picture Credits

Albert Meyer (courtesy of Creativ Werbeagentur) 2; Carmarthenshire Archives Service 28; Getty
Images 7, 15, 18, 23, 26, 29, 32, 33, 35, 42, 44, 45, 47, 48, 50, 51, 53, 54, 55, 56, 58, 60, 61, 62, 65, 66, 67,
69, 70, 71, 72, 73, 75, 77, 79, 81, 82, 84, 85, 87, 91; Hampshire County Council 25; Jane Holderness-
Roddam 36; Bob Langrish 37; Oldham Evening Chronicle 5; Mike Powell /Allsport 65

CONTENTS

ACKNOWLEDGEMENTS

Way back in 2008 after the Beijing Games, my good friend and fellow croquet player Alec Thomas came up with the idea of a book on British Olympic gold medallists through the ages. We began to research every last one of them (many scantly documented and some of them extremely dull!) and I took the idea to my old friends at Stacey International Publishing. Immediately, the focus sharpened and I began to write in earnest about the most interesting and intriguing of our outstanding athletes, living legends and eccentric heroes. I joined the International Society of Olympic Historians and Alec took a back seat but, without his early graft and encouragement, that first edition would never have seen the light of day.

My husband, Jonathan Edwards – not the triple jumper but, yes, a distant cousin of Eddie 'the Eagle' – has been my mainstay throughout and without his practical and moral support I would have long ago thrown in the towel. My brother, Alan Kittermaster, another keen sportsman, was also a source of help and encouragement.

I am enormously grateful to Bill Mallon and Jeroen Heijmans of the International Society of Olympic Historians who provided invaluable information and patiently answered my questions. Tony Bijkerk, Secretary-General of the ISOH and a walking encyclopaedia of the Olympic Games, took the time to read the first manuscript and correct my errors. I cannot sufficiently thank him for his efforts to ensure the accuracy of this work; his contribution improved it immeasurably, and his continued interest I value. If errors remain, they are no fault of his.

Although this revised, expanded and updated edition owes much to the continued encouragement of friends and family, as well as the advice and editorial skills of my co-director Peter Harrigan, I will always be deeply indebted to Tom Stacey, who believed in the book from the first.

KC

FOREWORD BY SIR CHRIS HOY, MBE

It is a huge honour to represent one's country at the Olympics, and an incredible opportunity for an athlete to take part in one of the greatest sporting events in the world.

As many British athletes continue their journey towards the London 2012 Olympics and prepare for the unique experience of competing in a home Games, this book celebrates a wealth and diversity of British sporting talent and achievement.

British Olympic Heroes features many contemporary and deservedly well-known names. It also includes figures from the past like Launceston Elliot, the first British Olympian, who combined Olympic success in one-handed weightlifting with rope-climbing, the discus and the 100 metres. And John Boland, who arrived at the 1896 Games as a spectator and ended up winning the singles and doubles tennis events.

The biographies document the important details and highlights of each athlete's career, but the book is also full of amusing anecdotes and little-known facts: did you know that the great all-rounder Max Woosnam beat Charlie Chaplin at table tennis playing with a butter knife, or that Kitty Godfree swapped her prizes to buy a sports car, or that Allan Wells was the first Olympic athlete to wear lycra shorts?

My own sporting heroes – Gavin Hastings, Graeme Obree and Chris Boardman – are an important source of inspiration and help spur me on to achieve my goals. I hope that today's aspiring athletes will read and enjoy this book and draw from it the inspiration to add to Britain's fantastic Olympic medal-winning achievements.

Chris Hoy

INTRODUCTION

Great Britain is one of only five countries to have competed in every Summer Olympic Games of the modern era, and one of only three to attend every Winter Games. In all, more than five hundred Britons have been awarded one or more gold medals. The exact figure depends on whether one includes the early curiosities such as Art and Alpinism (as we do) and the Second International Olympic Games (also known as the Intercalated Games). These Games were held in Athens in 1906, the Greeks having unilaterally decreed that the Olympics were their birthright and should be held permanently in Athens. The Greek Olympic Committee declared that the 1904 Games had been so badly run that they would show the world how things should be done. Thus three Games were held in the space of eight years. The IOC at first recognised the 1906 Games, but later expunged the results from the record books. A second interim Games was scheduled for 1914, but Baron de Coubertin, founder of the modern Olympics, won the battle to ensure that they were hosted by a different country each time.

It was not until 1906 that the now familiar sequence of gold, silver and bronze medals were awarded, so the athletes from the early Games included here as 'gold medallists' received either a silver medal, a small sum of money or a piece of art, and a laurel wreath. But they won, and that is what counts.

Those featured here are not necessarily the most famous. They are, rather, the most arresting, whose sporting and private lives have been inspiring and impressive or sometimes downright incredible. Our coverage in fact includes a larger number of Olympians in that the medal is sometimes shared between pairs or teams, as in swimming, rowing, sailing, skating or bobsledding. It's a curious fact that the British do rather better than average in sports that involve sitting down, lying down or going backwards! We are in the top four countries in the all-time medal tables for sailing (first), track cycling (second), rowing (third) and equestrian eventing (fourth). We come sixth in the shooting medal tables, but we *are* third in the athletics table, so we can run, jump and throw with the best of them.

Many of Britain's gold medallists have left a lasting legacy. Some made barely a ripple. Some single-mindedly devoted their lives to sport with the one goal of winning for their country; others found themselves on the podium quite by chance. In this book you will find those like Seb Coe, Chris Hoy and Kelly Holmes – household names today – inspiring countless others. There are those like Tommy Green and the Doherty brothers who overcame adversity and emerged victorious, and others like Max Woosnam whose truly amazing prowess is all but forgotten today. A few particularly unlikely participants appear, such as John Boland who went to Athens as a spectator and ended up the victor in two tennis events. And, in spite of its title, this book would be the poorer without at least a passing mention of our spectacular failures and unlucky losers, like Eddie 'the Eagle' Edwards and Philip Plater.

Since the first modern Olympics Games of 1896, various sports have disappeared from the Olympic programme, and with every new Games other sports are added. In many of the early events the British did extremely well. It was not difficult to foresee a British victory in the 1908 rackets competition, since no other nation took part. Nor in the cricket in 1900, which though ostensibly between Britain and France featured only a couple of players on either side who were not British. At those early Games, Britain managed to pick up a couple of gold medals in the water motor sports, two silvers in the rugby, and two of each in the tug-of-war. Polo, real tennis, golf and lacrosse accounted for a further 30 medals. Britain won three gold medals in Art, a 'sport' for many years included. One of these was for Town Planning in 1932. And the Everest expedition of 1922 earned the team, which included Mallory, an Alpine gold medal in 1924. A full list of all British gold medallists can be found at the end of the book.

An international group of dedicated Olympic researchers, led by American Bill Mallon, has compiled an Olympic database (the product of 60 man-years' work, they reckon) of great thoroughness and authority and their statistics are noted when they differ from the IOC's official lists. The leaders of this group went on to found the International Society of Olympic Historians in 1991.

The 2012 London Olympics are the third time Britain will have hosted the Games. New heroes are waiting in the wings and many of them, I have no doubt, will be British.

Kitty Carruthers, April 2012

OLYMPIC TIMELINE

Venue (Summer) (Winter)	Year	Notable Events
	1892	Baron Pierre de Coubertin puts plans for International Olympic Committee to delegates from 12 countries.
	1894	First session of IOC awards first Olympic Games to Athens.
Athens	1896	Games open with approximately 245 male competitors from 14 nations. Olympic hymn played during opening ceremony. Winners awarded silver medals and laurel wreaths.
Paris	1900	First women compete. Most winners do not receive medals and some receive cash prizes. Many never know they competed in Olympics. Longest croquet tournament in history (21 days) with smallest audience (a solitary Englishman).
St Louis	1904	Originally awarded to Chicago then moved to St Louis to be part of the Louisiana Purchase Exposition. Games take four and a half months to complete. Women allowed to box for the only time until 2012.
Athens	1906	The 2nd International Olympic Games. Unhappy with the organisation of the previous Games and claiming the Olympics as their birthright, the Greeks hold 'interim' Games. Winners receive gold, silver and bronze medals; IOC publishes the results, but in 1949 rule that the Games should not count.
London	1908	Games scheduled to be held in Rome, but Mt Vesuvius erupts. Within ten months the English build Shepherd's Bush stadium. Games launched with the support of the Franco-British Exhibition. First official opening ceremony to have parade of nations, but the wrong flags are flown causing the Swedes to storm out and the Americans to refuse to dip their flag to the royal box. Ray Ewry of USA wins eight gold medals. Dorando Pietri collapses in marathon and is carried across the line, forfeiting his medal but becoming a celebrity.
Stockholm	1912	First use of electronic timing and public address system. Jim Thorpe breaks records in first pentathlon and in decathlon, but is later stripped of medals for taking part in professional baseball. His medals posthumously rewarded.

Greco-Roman light-heavyweight finalists wrestle for 9 hours before contest is declared a double loss (or double win, however you look at it).

| | 1914 | Coubertin designs Olympic flag. |

Antwerp 1920 War prevents 1916 Games and Germany and other aggressor nations banned. Olympic flag flown for first time. Olympic Oath taken for the first time by Victor Boin. Coubertin outlines Olympic Charter. Ice hockey and figure skating included for only time in Summer Games.

1921 Coubertin introduces Olympic motto, 'citius, altius, fortius' (faster, higher, stronger).

Chamonix 1924 'International Winter Sports Weeks' held prior to Summer Games, and later designated the first Winter Olympics. Britain wins 4 medals – a record.

Paris Summer Games have first radio broadcast and closing ceremony. Johnny Weissmuller (Tarzan) and Dr Spock win medals.

St Moritz 1928 Winter Games begin in blizzard and end in 25°C. Several events cancelled for lack of ice and snow. Sonja Henie wins skating gold aged 15.

Amsterdam Generally harmonious Games; women allowed to compete in track and field for first time, until some girls collapse after finishing the 800m. Calls are made to remove the event from Olympic programme and as a result it does not reappear on programme until 1960. Olympic flame burns for duration of Games. Opening ceremony sees Greece enter first and hosts last, setting precedent for all future Games.

Lake Placid 1932 Warm weather again adversely affects Games. Eddie Eagan, boxing medallist in 1920, wins bobsleigh to become only man to win Winter and Summer medals. Ski instructors banned as professionals so Swiss and Austrians refuse to compete.

Los Angeles Fewer athletes but record crowds attend. First Games to make a profit. Male athletes housed in dedicated Village for first time, and women stay in luxury hotel. Podium, award ceremony and flag raising introduced. Prohibition lifted allowing athletes to imbibe alcohol. Photo-finish cameras introduced. Swedish equestrian loses dressage silver medal for 'clicking' to his horse.

Garmisch-Partenkirchen	1936	Last year in which Winter and Summer Games held in same country. Alpine skiing makes its first appearance. 28 nations take part.
Berlin	1936	Jewish groups call for boycott, but fail. Black athlete Jesse Owens wins four gold medals — one in the eye for Hitler. Torch relay introduced. First television coverage and wire service for results. Leni Riefenstahl's film *Olympia* released. German equestrian von Wangeheim breaks collarbone in steeplechase, falls again under horse, but remounts, goes clear, and Germany win team gold.
	1938	Japan returns Olympic Games to IOC because of war in China. IOC awards 1940 Games to Garmisch-Partenkirchen and Helsinki.
	1940	WWII causes cancellation of Winter and Summer Games.
	1944	War again prevents Games taking place.
St Moritz	1948	28 countries compete. Two American hockey teams turn up claiming to be official representatives. Olympic flag stolen twice.
London		Germany and Japan banned, but record 59 nations take part. First political defections occur. Fanny Blankers-Koen wins four gold medals on track. First Stoke Mandeville Games held, blueprint for Paralympics.
Oslo	1952	Olympic flame lit in home fireplace of skiing pioneer Sondre Norheim. Flame also lit atop Pallastunturi in Finland by rays of midnight sun and later combined with flame from Olympia. Torch relay conducted by 94 participants on skis.
Helsinki		Highly successful Games lead to calls for them to be held permanently in Scandinavia. Emil Zàtopek becomes only person to win 5,000m, 10,000m and marathon at same Olympics. Women allowed to enter open dressage event and Lis Hartel wins silver despite being paralysed below the knees.

Cortina d'Ampezzo	1956	First Winter Games to be televised. Torchbearer enters stadium on skates, falls and almost extinguishes flame. Soviet Union attends for first time and wins the most medals.
Melbourne & Stockholm	1956	First Games to be held in southern hemisphere. Many nations boycott: Egypt, Iraq and Lebanon at Israeli-led invasion of Suez Canal, and the Netherlands, Spain and Switzerland at Soviet invasion of Hungary (45 Hungarians refuse to return home). West and East Germany enter combined team. Following idea submitted by young Chinese boy, closing ceremony is forever changed by mingling all competitors into one Olympic Family. Due to obstacles of quarantine and difficulties in transporting horses, equestrian events held in Stockholm and designated Equestrian Olympic Games.
Squaw Valley, USA	1960	Opening and closing ceremonies produced by Walt Disney. First Winter Games to have dedicated athletes' Village and to have computerised results. Women take part in speed skating for first time.
Rome		Rome finally gets its chance and holds many events at ancient sites. Pope watches the canoeing from his summer residence. Yugoslavia wins football tournament after qualifying on a coin toss. First official Paralympic Games take place.
Innsbruck	1964	Warm weather causes lack of snow and Austrian army imports snow and ice. Luge competitor killed in pre-race run.
Tokyo		First Games held in Asia. Torchbearer born in Hiroshima on day atomic bomb dropped. Politics cause South Africa to be banned and Indonesia and North Korea to withdraw. Computerised scoring introduced to Summer Games. Ukrainian Larysa Latynina brings medal tally to 18, nine of them gold. Two cyclists set record for standing still (21:57 minutes), while waiting for the right moment to sprint home.
	1967	IOC draws up list of banned substances.
Grenoble	1968	First Games to be broadcast in colour. Organising Committee sell TV rights for US$2m. Jean-Claude Killy sweeps all men's alpine skiing events.

Mexico City		Student riots and Black Power activist athletes cause disruption. Altitude causes problems for athletes in endurance events. First drug testing introduced, as well as sex testing. Swedish entrant tests positive for alcohol. First woman lights Olympic cauldron. First truly synthetic track used. Dick Fosbury revolutionises high jump and Bob Beamon sets astonishing 8.9m long jump record.
Sapporo	1972	Issue of amateurism vs professionalism clouds Games. First and only Spanish slalom winner. Ard Schenk of Netherlands wins three gold medals in speedskating.
Munich		Largest Games yet, intended to celebrate peace, but 11 Israeli athletes murdered by Palestinian terrorists. Mark Spitz wins seven gold medals. Lasse Viren falls in 10,000m final but wins. Teenage gymnast Olga Korbut becomes a star.
Innsbruck	1976	Citizens of Denver refuse to host Games, so Innsbruck takes them for the second time, and two Olympic flames are lit. First Winter Paralympics held.
Montreal		Poor budgeting causes long-lasting debt to Canadians, but Games run smoothly. Games boycotted by 22 African nations in protest at All Blacks tour of South Africa. Nadia Comaneci of Romania awarded seven perfect scores in gymnastics. Japan's Shun Fujimoto breaks leg in floor exercise but competes in the rings, dislocating knee on dismount.
Lake Placid	1980	The Summer Games boycott overshadows the event. Liechtenstein becomes smallest country to produce a gold medallist. American Eric Heiden wins all men's speedskating events, taking five gold medals.
Moscow		US President Carter leads mass boycott over Soviet invasion of Afghanistan. Drug-enhanced Soviets win 11 of 13 swimming events and all 54 rowers win a medal. Coe and Ovett face off in the 800m and 1,500m. Both gold- and silver-medal winning coxless pairs are identical twins.
Sarajevo	1984	Games go without hitch despite impending civil war. Torvill and Dean awarded perfect score in ice dancing.
Los Angeles		First Games to be staged without government finance make US$223m profit. 140 nations take part. China sends first team for 52 years. Soviet Union stages

revenge boycott. John Williams composes 'Olympic Fanfare and Theme'. Carl Lewis wins 100m, 200m, long jump and 4x100m relay. Professionals allowed to play football if they have not taken part in World Cup.

Calgary   1988   First Winter Games to last 16 days. Eddie 'the Eagle' Edwards makes the headlines. The Jamaican bobsleigh team surprisingly qualify and are later made heroes by the film *Cool Runnings*. Yvonne van Gennip of Netherlands beats drug-enhanced DDR competitors and wins three gold medals.

Seoul   South Korea adopts democracy to host Games. North Korea, Cuba, Ethiopia and Nicaragua boycott. Canadian Ben Johnson tests positive for drugs and is disqualified.

Albertville   1992   Last Winter Games held the same year as Summer Games. Events spread out over the Savoie region. Germany competes as a single nation for the first time since 1964.

Barcelona   South Africa re-enters after 32 years in the wilderness. After fall of Communism, Yugoslavia banned because of military aggression, but individuals allowed to enter. Estonia and Latvia make first appearance since 1936, and Lithuania since 1928. Other ex-Soviet countries compete as the 'Unified Team'. The 10,000m race sees first black African female gold medallist. Men's basketball allows professionals and the American 'dream team' average 117 points per game, and never call a timeout.

Lillehammer   1994   Czechoslovakia divides and Slovakia makes first Olympic appearance. Games said to be 'Best Olympic Winter Games' ever. Women's figure skating in uproar after Nancy Kerrigan is assaulted by Tonya Harding's ex-husband.

Atlanta   1996   Over 10,000 athletes from 197 nations take part. Major organisational problems occur, particularly in transport. Terrorist bomb kills two and injures 111 at Atlanta concert. Football teams are allowed three professionals regardless and Nigeria beat Argentina in the final. Hubert Raudashl of Austria becomes the first person to compete in nine Olympics.

Nagano	1998	Record 2,180 athletes and 72 nations take part. New world records set in speed skating due to the innovative clap skate. Norway's Björn Daehlie wins three golds and one silver, bringing his Olympic medal tally to twelve, of which eight are gold.
Sydney	2000	More than 10,600 athletes take part, and the authorities crack down on doping. East Timor takes part despite not being recognised by the IOC, bringing the number of nations participating to 199. The Bahamas becomes the smallest country to win a team event, in the 4x100m women's relay. Haile Gebreselassie of Ethiopia wins photo-finish 10,000m race. Steve Redgrave wins fifth gold medal in rowing.
Salt Lake City	2002	Games marred by scandal over claims that IOC officials received bribes in 1999 to award them to Salt Lake City. Controversy between Canada and Russia over the pairs figure skating after French judge pressurised to mark up the Russians. Both pairs eventually awarded gold at a second ceremony.
	2003	Vancouver awarded the 2010 Winter Games.
Athens	2004	Organisers silence critics by being ready on time. Kelly Holmes becomes first British woman to win two gold medals.
	2005	London awarded the 2012 Games, becoming the first city officially to host them three times. IOC calls for Games to be limited to a maximum of 10,500 athletes.
Turin	2006	Italy awarded second Winter Games and adopts the motto 'Passion lives here'. A record 80 nations take part. Official mascots are a female snowball and a male ice cube. Ethiopia and Madagascar send one athlete each.
Beijing	2008	China hosts $40b Olympics in spite of human rights record as IOC warns against politicising the Games. Almost 11,000 athletes attend and receive the largest television audience in Olympic history. 'Bird's Nest' stadium takes five years to build. Longest torch relay, lasting 130 days and covering 85,000 miles (taking in Mt Everest), encounters difficulties from protesters along the way. IOC reverses ban on Iraq's attendance. South African swimmer Natalie du Toit becomes first amputee to compete in Olympics. American Michael Phelps wins eight swimming

gold medals. Usain Bolt of Jamaica breaks three world records to become the world's fastest man. Britain's Chris Hoy wins three gold medals in cycling. China pull out the stops with spectacular pyrotechnic closing ceremony with 90,000 audience and 1.5 billion viewers. Mayor of Beijing hands Olympic flag to Boris Johnson, Mayor of London, and David Beckham kicks football into crowd.

Vancouver   2010   2,600 athletes participate from 82 nations. Canada beats the Soviet Union's 1976 record of Winter Olympic gold medals by one – taking 14 in all. Amy Williams wins skeleton gold medal, the first British individual Winter gold since 1980, and is awarded the MBE.

2012   Greek actress Ino Menegaki acting as High Priestess kindles the sacred flame using the sun's rays and a concave mirror among the ruins of the Temple of Hera in Ancient Olympia (pictured below), to begin its journey to London. Flame arrives in UK on 18 May, and the first leg of the torch relay is run by gold medallist Ben Ainslie.

'The flame that we kindle here from the pure rays of the sun is a powerful symbol of the traditions and values that underlie our movements. ... the torchbearers who carry this flame to London will spread the message of sport's capacity to promote peace and to make our world a better place,' says Jacques Rogge in his last address at this ceremony as President of the IOC.

BRITISH OLYMPIC HEROES

A selection of the greatest (and most interesting)
gold medallists from 1896 to 2008

Launceston Elliot
1896 Athens
Weightlifting, One-Handed Lift

Launceston Elliot was the first British Olympic Champion. Not content with winning Britain's first ever Olympic medal in the one-handed lift, he entered the 100m sprint, where he came third, the heavyweight wrestling, coming fourth and the rope climbing competition. Then, at the 1900 Games, when no weightlifting events were held, he entered for the discus.

A member of the aristocratic Scottish family headed by Lord Minto, Elliot's strange family history warrants a mention. His father's first wife fell to her death from a hotel balcony in Australia in unexplained circumstances, whereupon his father married the hotel receptionist. He then married again (though what happened to the receptionist is not recorded), and Launceston was the fruit of this third marriage, conceived in Launceston, Tasmania, and born in India.

A man of superb physique, Elliot took to weightlifting early and at the age of only 16 entered the first British Championships in London's Piccadilly. By the time he was 19 he had succeeded in winning the event.

When he went to Athens in 1896, Elliot's handsome features and muscular build attracted much attention, even offers of marriage. The official Olympic report described him as being of 'uncommon beauty . . . impressive stature, tall, well-proportioned'. The weightlifting contest boiled down to a contest between Elliot and Viggo Jensen, a Dane. The rules were somewhat hazy, and after the two-handed event both men had lifted 111.5 kgs. The judges, however, preferred Jensen's style and placed him first. But in the one-handed lift, Elliot completed a lift of 71 kgs, 13 kgs more than Jensen could manage.

Before turning professional in 1905 Elliot had set four new world records at the 1899 Amateur Championships. His professional career became somewhat more colourful when he turned to the music hall stage. He and a partner would perform as gladiators, and at the end of the show Elliot's *pièce de résistance* was to support a bicycle and rider at each end of a pole across his mighty shoulders, turning in ever-faster circles until the riders were swinging horizontally. He was fond of including pretty girls in his act, and at one stage had 12 stunners to assist him. His wife would accompany him everywhere on tour, largely, one suspects, to repel the advances of his entourage and audience.

He retired in 1920 and farmed in Essex for several years before settling in Australia with his wife, where he died of spine cancer in 1930.

John Boland
1896 Athens
Lawn Tennis, Doubles & Singles

The reluctant sportsman, John Boland, hand on hip, in 1896. His German partner, Fritz Traun, leans forward to talk to their Greek opponents.

John Boland was a most unlikely Olympian. He turned up to watch and ended by winning both the singles and the doubles tennis tournaments.

The son of a Dublin baker and a man of broad erudition, he studied at the Catholic University School in Dublin, Edgbaston Oratory, and the Universities of Oxford, London and Bonn. He was a fine cricketer and very good at tennis as well as being a keen rugby player, but had little top-class competitive experience.

While at Oxford, he had become friendly with Thrasyvoalos Manaos, Secretary of the 1896 Organising Committee, who invited him to the Games in Athens. Expecting only to spectate, he was reluctantly persuaded by Manaos to enter the tennis tournament. In spite of having no international experience, and wearing leathersoled shoes with heels, he borrowed a racket and won not only the singles title, but the doubles as well, with a German whose partner had suddenly withdrawn.

Boland was called to the Bar in 1897, became Member of Parliament for South Kerry from 1900 to 1918, and was General Secretary of the Catholic Truth Society for 21 years. He was an ardent proponent of Irish independence and the Irish language, and helped found the National University of Ireland, which promoted the Irish language as an essential examination subject.

The first Irish-born Olympic medallist, he died in London on St Patrick's Day 1958, at the age of 88.

Laurie and Reggie Doherty
1900 Paris and 1908 London

Laurie   Lawn Tennis, Singles & Doubles (1900)
Reggie   Lawn Tennis, Doubles & Mixed Doubles (1900)
*   Lawn Tennis, Doubles (1908)*

The Doherty brothers were possibly the greatest doubles partnership in the history of tennis and dominated the game at the turn of the century. Between them they won eight Wimbledon doubles and nine singles titles, three US titles and six Olympic medals, and were unbeaten in their five Davis Cup rubbers. Their record is all the more remarkable since both were plagued by ill health from boyhood and frequently competed in the teeth of medical advice. Spectators at the 1898 Wimbledon final, however, would hardly have known that they suffered from respiratory difficulties, for the brothers played 45 games in 55 minutes. Known as Big Do and Little Do, the handsome pair drew large crowds to their matches and were said to cause women to swoon by the courtside.

Laurie, three years younger than 'Big Do', is generally reckoned to be the better of the two, and the finest British player of all time after Fred Perry. In 1903 he became the first foreign male player to win the US singles title, taking the Wimbledon singles and doubles titles and the Davis Cup in the same year, making him the first true 'Grand Slam' champion.

The two men entered the singles, doubles and mixed doubles tournaments of the 1900 Olympic Games. After winning the doubles in three straight sets, Laurie was scheduled to meet his brother in the semi-finals of the singles, but Reggie conceded a walkover and Laurie went on to beat the Irishman, Harold Mahoney, in the final. The two met again in the mixed doubles semi-final, Laurie partnered by the American Marion Jones and Reggie by Chattie Cooper. Reggie and Chattie went on to win the competition without dropping a set.

By 1906, the health of both players had deteriorated and they were so exhausted in chasing their ninth successive Wimbledon doubles title that their tearful mother begged them to give it up. Laurie dutifully took heed, and turned to

The dashing Doherty brothers, Reggie reclining and Laurie on the right.

golf instead, but Reggie entered the Olympics again in 1908, where he won his second doubles gold medal, this time with George Hillyard. He continued to play, taking two titles at the South African Championships in 1909, but the effort was to prove too great a strain, and he died the following year.

In spite of his frailty, Laurie joined the Royal Naval Reserve in 1914 but the rigours of life in the Anti-Aircraft branch took their inevitable toll. He was invalided out and after a long illness died in 1919.

The Dohertys found time during their brief and busy lives to co-author a book on tennis instruction, *RF & HL Doherty on Lawn Tennis*, a rare and much sought-after title. Their good looks and popularity at the turn of the century did much to revive the fortunes of the All England Lawn Tennis and Croquet Club, which at the time was barely making a profit on the annual Championships. In 1931 their brother, the Rev. William, donated the Doherty Memorial Gates to Wimbledon, a fitting tribute to such a talented and influential pair.

Charlotte (Chattie) Cooper
1900 Paris
Lawn Tennis, Ladies' Singles & Mixed Doubles

Born in London in 1870, Chattie Cooper has entered the record books for more than her two wins in Paris in 1900: she was the first woman to become an Olympic champion, the oldest winner of the Wimbledon singles title, and

the longest-lived Olympian. In 1900 she beat the French champion, Hélène Prévost, in straight sets to win the singles and then took the doubles gold medal with Reggie Doherty as her partner. She

Chattie Cooper in her prime in 1900.

also won a silver medal in the mixed doubles with Max Woosnam.

Slender but strong, Cooper cut an impressive figure on the courts in her ankle-length skirts and high collars, but the restrictive Edwardian-style attire failed to stop her successfully competing until well into her 50s. In all, she won five Wimbledon singles titles, the last at the age of almost 38, having returned to the game after an absence to raise her family. She was married at the late (for her era) age of 30 to fellow tennis player, Alfred Sterry, who became President of the Lawn Tennis Association. Their daughter, Gwen, was also a talented player and was part of the British Wightman Cup team. It is possible that Cooper might have won more medals had she been allowed to compete in the first Games, but in 1896 only men were allowed to enter.

Henry Taylor
1906 Athens and 1908 London
Swimming, 1-Mile Freestyle (1906)
Swimming, 400m Freestyle, 1,500m Freestyle & 4x200m Freestyle Relay (1908)

Born into poverty and orphaned at an early age, Henry Taylor went on to become one of Britain's most successful swimmers, winning a record eight Olympic medals in four successive Games. His tally of three gold medals at one Olympics is a British achievement matched only by Chris Hoy in 2008. Semi-literate and only 5'5" tall, Taylor's prodigious talent earned him 35 trophies and more than 300 medals during his career, yet he died in obscurity.

Brought up and trained by his elder brother Bill, Taylor learned to swim in the canal in his home town of Oldham. At the age of seven he entered his first race at the local baths, beating rivals much older than himself. He trained hard and was soon noticed and selected for the Games in 1906 where he won the 1-mile freestyle gold medal. Later the same year he set a world record for the 880 yards and was an obvious choice for the 1908 Games. There he lost only one race, the second 400m semi-final, but powered home in the final ten seconds ahead of the field, going on

to finish first in the 1,500m final and winning his third gold medal in the 4x200m relay.

Four years later in Stockholm, Taylor anchored the 4x200m bronze-winning freestyle relay team. The 1916 Games were cancelled because of the war and Taylor joined the Navy, but he returned for his fourth Games in 1920 and again won a bronze medal with the relay team. During the war Taylor achieved the status of 'Champion Swimmer' by swimming round the entire fleet, then anchored at Scapa Flow – quite an achievement given the size of the British fleet at the time and the choppy conditions. He also represented England at water polo.

In spite of his small stature, Taylor cut a fine figure in his handmade silk swimming costume, complete with 'modesty slip' – a sort of knotted handkerchief worn like a thong.

At the age of 41 he retired from competitive swimming. Never adept at managing his finances, he pawned most of his numerous trophies to buy an inn, but failed to make a success of it and the silverware was lost to him forever. He took a job as an attendant at Oldham's Chadderton Baths and at the age of 65 died impoverished and forgotten, a sad end for a man once hailed as 'Britain's Greatest Amateur Swimmer'.

A measure of belated recognition was accorded in 2002 when a blue plaque to him was unveiled at Chadderton Baths, where some of his trophies have been gathered together and displayed.

Taylor with his impressive display of trophies.

John Jacob Astor, 1st Baron Astor of Hever

1908 London

Rackets, Doubles

When John Jacob Astor won his rackets gold medal in the London Olympics in 1908 he still had both legs. In later life, he was still winning squash tournaments with one leg!*

Born in New York in 1886 into the Astor banking family, John Jacob came as a child to England, where he and his family were naturalised in 1899. After Eton and a short period at Oxford, he took a commission in the Life Guards, serving as ADC to Lord Hardinge, then Viceroy of India. At the outbreak of war he returned to active duty, distinguishing himself by his bravery. In September 1918, he was wounded in 14 places and his right leg was amputated. To take his mind off his injuries, his father gave him Hever Castle.

Inheriting a fortune on the death of his father in 1919, he sought a more meaningful role in life. He was elected to Parliament as Unionist member for Dover in 1922, a seat he held until 1945, but is perhaps best known for his stewardship of *The Times* newspaper, of which he was chief proprietor from 1922 to 1966. He famously sponsored Colonel John Hunt's expedition by which Hillary and Tensing conquered Everest in 1952.

At Eton, as well as opening the batting for the cricket team in 1904 and 1905, he won the public schools rackets championship with M. W. Bovill in 1905. In 1908, he won the Army singles rackets championship, and the doubles with Lord Somers.

The two 1908 Olympics rackets events were contested only by British players. Astor won gold in the doubles, with Vane Pennell, and bronze in the singles. After the war and in spite of his tin leg, as he called it, he continued to play, winning the parliamentary squash rackets competition in 1926 and 1927. He also played cricket, tennis and golf, and became President of the MCC in 1937.

Lord Astor, notwithstanding his wealth, power and achievements, lived frugally and unassumingly. In later life he took up painting, and died in 1971.

Lord Astor in Life Guards' uniform as ADC to Lord Hardinge.

---

* There *was* a one-legged Olympian. American George Eyser won three gold medals, two silvers and a bronze in the 1904 gymnastics wearing a wooden leg.

Wyndham Halswelle
1908 London
Athletics, 400m

The lonely figure of Wyndham Halswelle as he wins the 400m in a walkover. His victory prompted one newspaper to offer the headline 'Halswelle That Ends Well'.

Wyndham Halswelle was a first-class sprinter and the winner of Scotland's first Olympic gold medal. It was unfortunate that his victory should have been achieved in such controversial circumstances, and that he should be remembered largely for being the only man in Olympic history to win in a walkover. Although London-born, Halswelle took the nationality of his Scottish grandfather, General Nathaniel Gordon. He excelled in athletics at Charterhouse School and Sandhurst, then took a commission in the Highland Light Infantry, who were sent in 1902 to fight the Boer War. His athletic ability was recognised while in South Africa, and when the regiment returned the following year Halswelle took up running seriously. Having won races in the Army and the AAA, he became part of the squad for the 1906

Games, taking a silver medal in the 400m and bronze in the 800m. That year, too, he achieved the impressive feat of winning the 100, 220, 440 and 880 yards races in a single day.

In the run-up to the 1908 Games, Halswelle succeeded in setting world and British records in the 300 and 440 yds. In qualifying for the finals of the 400m at the Games themselves, he set an Olympic record of 48.4. But the final itself was to prove a messy affair. Alongside Halswelle were three Americans, and the race was to be run without lanes. Coming off the final bend, Halswelle was in third place, poised to pass in the last straight, as was his habit. As he did so, Carpenter, the American in second place, ran wide, elbowing Halswelle almost off the track. The umpire cried 'Foul!' and the race was declared void. Blocking at the time was allowed in American races, but not in the Olympics, and Carpenter was disqualified. The race was to be rerun in lanes. Siding with the disgruntled Carpenter, the two remaining American athletes refused to take part, and Halswelle won in a walkover, with a sedate time of 50.2. The only positive outcomes of this debacle were that from then on all 400m races were run in lanes, and the Amateur Athletic Federation was founded to standardise rules and prevent similar mishaps.

Halswelle, however, was disenchanted and ran only one more race before retiring. He was killed by a sniper bullet at the Battle of Neuve Chapelle in March 1915.

Paulo Radmilovic

1908 London, 1912 Stockholm, 1920 Antwerp
Water Polo (1908, 1912 & 1920), Swimming 4x200m Freestyle Relay (1908)

Born in 1886, Paulo Radmilovic (known as Paul or Raddy) was one of Britain's greatest Olympians, and has often been dubbed 'Wales's greatest ever sportsman'. In an Olympic career which spanned 22 years he competed in six consecutive Games – the first Briton to do so, and the last until Tessa Sanderson in 1996 – and his record of four gold medals in three successive Olympic Games was only broken when Sir Steve Redgrave won his historic fifth gold at Sydney in 2000. He is also one of only a handful of Olympians to have won medals in two different disciplines.

Born in Cardiff of Croatian-Irish descent, Radmilovic's family relocated to Weston-Super-Mare when he was a child, and there he began swimming in the waters of the Bristol Channel. From an early age he showed great promise as an all-round sportsman, his talents reaching beyond swimming and water polo to football, athletics, boxing and (as a scratch player) golf. When he was only 15 years old he began his international career as a member of the Welsh national water polo team.

Radmilovic made his Olympic debut at the 1906 Intercalated Games, but he failed to make the medal table in the three swimming events he entered. In 1908, he attended the London Olympics as part of the British men's water polo team, as well being recruited at the last minute for the 4x200m freestyle relay team. Within the space of two days he won gold medals in both events, scoring twice in the final of the water

polo and becoming the first Welshman to win an Olympic gold.

Returning for the 1912 Games in Stockholm, Radmilovic won his third gold medal, captaining the British water polo team which beat the Austrians by a resounding 8-0 in the final.

On his next appearance, at the Antwerp Olympics in 1920, he won his fourth gold medal with the British water polo squad. In a tight final against the home side, Radmilovic, again the captain, scored three minutes from time to put the British 3-2 ahead. As the final whistle went, the highly-incensed Belgian crowd started a riot and the victorious team had to be escorted from the pool under armed guard.

Paulo Radmilovic (middle row, right) with Great Britain's gold medal-winning water polo team in 1920.

Paris 1924, and there was Radmilovic again, now aged 38, but the water polo team failed to make the medals. The same disappointment faced them in 1928 in Amsterdam, Radmilovic's last Olympic appearance.

Although his four gold medals gained him recognition for water polo, Radmilovic's swimming career was also a long and illustrious one: he won nine Amateur Swimming Association freestyle titles at various distances from 100 yards to five miles, the English Long Distance Championships in 1907 and 1925 and, in 1926, the English One Mile Championship.

His last victory came at the age of 43 in a 440 yards event, but even in his late seventies he continued to swim a quarter of a mile every day. When he retired from swimming, Radmilovic became the licensee of the Imperial Hotel in Weston-Super-Mare.

In 1967 he was inducted into the Swimming Hall of Fame, and 1993 into the Welsh Sports Hall of Fame. His achievements were further recognised in Wales with a plaque at the Cardiff International Pool, paid for by the 2012 London Olympics Committee and the Welsh Assembly and unveiled in 2008 on the 100th anniversary of his double-gold Olympic success. As part of this belated recognition, attempts were made to track down Radmilovic's Olympic medals, which went missing after his death in 1968 and subsequent family squabbles. Sadly, there is still no sign of them.

Curiously, in 1992 Guyana issued a set of postage stamps featuring Olympic gold medalists from the past. A $25 stamp shows Radmilovic in the water, his arms outstretched, with the caption 'Paul Radmilovic. GDR. 1920 Waterpolo (team)'. Does anyone have an explanation?

Madge Syers
1908 London
Figure Skating, Ladies

Florence 'Madge' Syers was the first female World and Olympic figure skating champion and, to date, the oldest.

Already known as the world's finest woman skater, she really caught the public's attention in 1902 when she came second in the World Championships. The fact that she had entered at all was a nasty shock to the organisers, the International Skating Union (ISU), who never dreamed that a woman would dare do so and had failed to take the precaution of banning them. It

was just as much of a shock that she came second.

Many thought she should have won, even the winner Ulrich Salchow, who reportedly handed her his gold medal as soon as it was presented to him. The International Skating Union immediately prohibited women from competing against men on the grounds that
   a) their long skirts made it hard for the judges to see their feet,
   b) pretty girls might be favoured by the judges,
   c) it is difficult to compare women with men.

Syers responded by shortening her skirts to mid-calf, thereby setting a trend.

One of 15 children born into a wealthy family in London, Madge Cave learned to skate, like many young society girls, at the Prince's Skating Rink in Knightsbridge. But unlike most of her contemporaries, she was a gifted athlete and took it seriously. At the same time as developing as a first-class skater, she was winning prizes for swimming and riding.

When she met Edgar Syers her life and her skating style changed dramatically. Edgar became her coach, encouraging her to adopt the freeflowing 'International' style of skating. In 1900 they married, and with the 1899 British

pairs championship gold medal under their belts, they came second in the first international pairs competition in Berlin. Though theirs was a formidable pairing, Madge's forte was individual figure skating.

In 1903 Madge won the first British singles championship, and the following year beat her husband to retain the title. In 1905 the ISU rescinded the ban on women competitors, and the next year introduced a separate event for ladies at the World Championships. Madge won in both 1906 and 1907, although it was not until 1920 that these two events were retroactively recognised as official.

Reigning supreme in the sport, she was the clear favourite for the 1908 Olympic women's singles title. The judges unanimously gave her firsts in the two elements of compulsory figures and free skating: she duly returned home with the gold medal. She and Edgar also won a bronze in the pairs event.

Soon after the Games, Madge's health began to fail and in 1917 at the age of 35 she died of influenza.

Madge and Edgar Syers at the Olympics in 1908.

Vivian Woodward
1908 London and 1912 Stockholm
Football

Viv Woodward, winner of 66 international caps and England's most prolific scorer during half a century, was almost certainly the greatest centre forward the country has ever produced. Known to his friends as Jack, and to his peers and the press as 'football's gentleman', Woodward was in his prime in an era when England led the world in football and he still appears in the list of top ten goalscorers and in the Football Association's top 100 players of all time. In 1908 he put eight of England's 15 goals past the French, a match tally never bettered by an England player, and the following year he scored four goals against Holland.

Woodward captained the England team to victory in two Olympic Games, scoring in every match. He was 33 when he led the English team in Stockholm. His leadership and sportsmanship endeared him to his teammates and earned him admiration within and beyond the world of football. One colleague, Bobby Steel of Clacton Town, described him as 'the finest centre forward I have ever seen. He was a gentleman and in all my association with him I never saw him commit

a foul or retaliate – and he did get some pastings.'

Born into a wealthy family and an architect by profession, he remained an amateur all his life. He started his career with Clacton Town FC, but his most prolific years were spent first with Tottenham Hotspur, and then with Chelsea. Although almost certain of selection for club and international matches, he often put work commitments first. As a first-class tennis player he sometimes preferred to be on the court rather than the pitch, and warned Spurs when he signed for them that he might be unavailable unless it was 'convenient'. He also excelled at cricket, captaining Essex when in his 40s, and seems to have been something of a whiz on rollerskates.

At the start of the First World War, Woodward joined the Army, enlisting in the 17th Service (Football) Battalion of the Middlesex Regiment. In 1915 his club, Chelsea, reached the final of the FA Cup, and he was given leave to take the place of the injured (and one-eyed) Bob Thompson. But when he heard that Thompson had recovered, with typical generosity and sportsmanship he refused to play, since Thompson had played in all previous cup matches and he had not. He was wounded in 1916, which put an end to his career. But he retained his links with the game, becoming a director of Chelsea from 1922 to 1930.

A superstar in his day, well before the days of celebrity sportsmen, Woodward died lonely and forgotten in 1954 in a London nursing home, a tragic end to one of England's finest.

Emil Voigt

1908 London

Athletics, 5 miles

Winner of the 5-mile race in 1908, Emil Voigt – who died in 1973 – still holds the title more than twenty-five years after his death, since the event was never held again. Voigt's further unique claim to fame is that he was the only vegetarian among the 2,023 Olympic entrants.

Born in Manchester of German parents, and described by the press as 'one of the most stylish runners ever seen on the path', Voigt was a well-travelled polyglot and a man of great energy and good cheer. Only 5 foot 5 inches tall and weighing eight stone, he eschewed meat, tobacco and alcohol, and was a lifelong proponent of a planned (vegetarian) diet, deep breathing and the benefits of massage in building up athletic prowess.

Although keen on cycling and football in his youth, running became Voigt's passion, and a versatile runner he was, winning races at anything between 800 metres and 10 miles. He had been thinking about retiring from athletics, but since the Olympics were to be held in his home country, he asked the officials if he could enter the trials at two weeks' notice. On a whim he asked to be entered in the 5-mile race (a distance he had never raced before) and at the last minute they agreed. He won the trial but had little time to prepare for the Games. He used the AAA 4-mile race in London as a warm-up and won it in style. But the training and racing had left him with painful feet, so he and his coach, keeping close counsel, decided he should take things easy until just before the Olympics.

In the heats in Manchester, Emil and six others lined up and set off. Tucked in the pack, he was jostled, tugged and rapped on the heels. So with a mile left to run, he decided to get out of harm's way. He turned on the turbos, went clear and won by 150 yards. But immediately he broke down, his foot muscles torn and an arch collapsed. It was assumed that he would take no further part.

Emil Voigt, winner of the last 5-mile Olympic event, poses for the camera in 1908.

That night Voigt took the train to London to see a specialist, who strapped the foot and built a special plaster of Paris arch support to go inside his shoe. On the day of the final, Voigt was unsure whether he could compete at all, let alone finish. Keeping his doubts to himself, he told the press he was 'in good trim', and lined up with the other nine finalists. Blanking out the pain, Voigt ran the race of his life. With his trademark spurt, in the last 700 yards he flashed past the field to win by 70 yards and break the world record – to the astonishment of the crowd, most of whom had never heard of him. Back home in Manchester, a huge crowd greeted him and carried him shoulder-high through the streets.

Putting thoughts of retirement behind him, Voigt continued to run at various distances, winning the 1-mile, 4-mile and 5-mile British championships. In 1911 he moved to Australia. He designed the cinder circuit in Melbourne, the first of its kind in the Southern Hemisphere. He soon became the Australian 6-mile champion and in 1913 the 2-mile record holder.

He also became a pioneer in broadcasting and founded his own radio station. Having long been interested in politics, he used his station to promote social justice and champion the underdog. This brought him under the scrutiny of the secret services in the UK and Australia as a suspected Communist, but, although he had leanings that direction, he was never a member of the Party.

In his 80s Voigt was still running several miles a day (up a volcano!), gliding, fishing and generally keeping happy and active. He ended his days in New Zealand, where he died at the age of 90.

Arnold Jackson
1912 Stockholm
Athletics, 1,500m

In 1912, the 21-year-old undergraduate Arnold Jackson came from behind to win what has been described as 'the greatest race ever run', breaking the world record and becoming the youngest ever Olympic 1,500m gold medallist.

Jackson, one of the dying breed of Edwardian gentlemen-amateurs, was not one to over-exert himself in practice, relying instead on his natural talent: his idea of training during the Olympics was to sit in the shade and ogle the good-looking lady tennis players, and after the 1,500m heats he decided his best preparation for the final would be to have a nap. An outsider, Jackson was not expected to beat the Americans, who at the time dominated the event. Coming off the final turn, three of the Americans, two of them mile and 1,500m world record holders, ran abreast, forcing Jackson to go wide. For 50 yards they ran together, but with a final burst Jackson pipped them at the post by a tenth of a second in a time of 3:56.8. So close was the finish that, for the only time in the 1912 Olympics, a photo-finish was needed to decide the outcome. It was the pinnacle of Jackson's short athletics career.

In all Jackson won only six major races, but he described his Olympic triumph as, 'a perfect day [against] capital fellow competitors'.

After studying law at Oxford (where he also rowed, and played hockey and football) 'Jackers' joined up during the First World War and served with great distinction. He became the British Army's youngest Brigadier General. He was awarded the DSO and three bars, the last for 'conspicuous gallantry and brilliant leadership'. He was mentioned in despatches nine times, but wounds received in action left him permanently lame and put an end to his sporting career.

Having changed his name to Arnold Nugent Strode Strode-Jackson, in 1921 he became a delegate at the Paris Peace Conference and was awarded the CBE.

Arnold Jackson leads the field in the final of the 1,500m in 1912.

Jackson practised as a barrister and was a member of the British Olympic Council in 1920. The following year he emigrated to America, becoming a US citizen in 1945. When his wife died in 1963, he returned to England where he passed away in 1972.

Kitty Godfree
1920 Antwerp
Lawn Tennis, Ladies' Doubles

The good-natured and gregarious Kitty Godfree (née Kathleen McKane) was the golden girl of British tennis in its heyday in the 1920s and '30s. Considered the finest woman tennis player the country has produced, she is one of its most successful Olympians, winning one gold, two silver and two bronze medals in successive Games in Antwerp and Paris. Her gold medal in Antwerp was won with Margaret McNair, and the mixed doubles silver medal with the legendary Max Woosnam. She had a terrific all-round game and was a particularly good volleyer (a rarity in those days), but her main strength lay in her mental toughness and gritty determination. The final of the 1924 Wimbledon Ladies' Singles against Helen Wills well demonstrated this: having lost the first set 4-6, and two breaks of serve and 40-15 down in the second, Kitty fought back to take the title 4-6, 6-4, 6-4, inflicting 'Little Miss Poker Face's' only defeat in nine Wimbledon appearances. 'This is the point where the English girl is so wonderful, where the grit of her country shows in her,' wrote the French tennis star Suzanne Lenglen at the time.

In 1926 she won the title again, and with it the prize of a £10 voucher and a bracelet worth five guineas from the jewellers Mappin & Webb. She later added this to other prize vouchers, and traded in her gems for a two-seater sports car.

Godfree was a remarkable all-round athlete, excelling not only at tennis but at also lacrosse, badminton, skating, cycling, croquet and cricket. At the age of nine, she cycled from London to Berlin – a 600-mile journey which was to her a mere 'outing'. She played lacrosse at International level and was four times the All England Badminton Champion. Such was her stamina that she was still playing competitive tennis in her nineties. At 92, as an honoured guest she attended the Seoul Olympics in 1988, the first time since 1924 that tennis had been included as a medal sport.

Godfree and her husband, Leslie, are the only married couple ever to win the Wimbledon Mixed Doubles title and, until Venus and Serena Williams, she and her sister were the only siblings to contest a Wimbledon Ladies' Doubles final. In her impressive Wimbledon career, Godfree won 111 of her 146 matches, and in 1925 became the first person to reach the singles finals of the French Championships and the US Championships in the same year.

Kitty Godfree is undoubtedly one of the best-remembered and popular tennis players of any era. Self-taught, modest about her manifold talents and amiable to all, she was an inspiration to many. As the BBC commentator Dan Maskell said in the introduction to her biography, 'Her victories sowed the seeds of Wimbledon wins. I feel she showed Britain the way in the world of tennis.'

The stylish Kitty Godfree at the Wimbledon Championships in 1926, where she beat Miss Lili de Alvarez of Spain in the final.

Henry Mallin
1920 Antwerp and 1924 Paris
Boxing, Middleweight

Harry Mallin, a London policeman, achieved the unique record of never having been beaten in 300 amateur fights.

His victory in the middleweight division at the Antwerp Games was relatively straightforward, but when he came to defend his title in Paris in 1924 extraordinary scenes ensued. Having cruised through the early rounds, he met local hero Roger Brousse in the quarter-finals. During the second round, with Mallin busy punishing the Frenchman with his powerful left, Brousse tried to bite him on the arm.

In the third and final round, Brousse succeeded in sinking his teeth into Mallin's chest, clean through his vest. At the end of the fight, which he figured he had won comfortably, Mallin protested to the referee and showed the teeth marks on his chest. A doctor examined him but declared that since Mallin's opponent had been wearing a gumshield on his lower set, it was impossible for him to have inflicted the wound. Brousse's supporters even declared that Mallin had bumped his chest against the Frenchman's gnashers, for he had a habit of snapping his jaw when throwing a punch. For the first time in his life, Mallin was declared the loser.

The British officials did nothing – neither the Earl of Cadogan, President of the British Olympic Association, nor the President of the International Amateur Boxing Federation. However, a Swedish official lodged a formal complaint on Mallin's behalf. Late that night and well into the following evening's scheduled events, the appeal jury examined the evidence. Eventually it was announced that Brousse had been disqualified. Brousse burst into tears, the French went berserk and fights broke out around the hall. Throughout the semi-final and final the disruptions and eruptions in the audience continued, and little was seen of Mallin's victory over fellow Briton Jack Elliott as he became the first man ever successfully to defend an Olympic boxing title. The *Daily Sketch* described Brousse as 'a man-eating expert' and other reports suggested he had sampled 'some of the unroasted human beef of Old England'.

During his astonishing career, Mallin not only won two Olympic gold medals, but five ABA titles as well, and when he retired after the Paris debacle no one had ever beaten him.

In 1936 he managed the British Olympic boxing team, and in 1937 gave the first ever television sports commentary in Britain on a fight at Alexandra Palace. He managed the British team again in 1952. His brother, Frederick, was also five-times British middleweight champion.

Henry Mallin retired undefeated after 300 amateur middleweight fights.

Max Woosnam
1920 Antwerp
Lawn Tennis, Men's Doubles

Max Woosnam was an outstandingly versatile sportsman, the like of whom the world will probably never see again. Here was a man, an amateur all his life, who acquired a degree and five Blues from Cambridge University, won Olympic gold and silver medals on the same day and a Wimbledon title, was captain of the England football team and Manchester City FC as well as of the British Davis Cup squad, made a perfect 147 break in a snooker match, was a scratch golfer, scored a century at Lords – oh, and fought in the trenches and rose to sit on the board of one of the biggest chemical companies in the world.

At Winchester, Woosnam played football and squash and captained the school's golf and cricket teams. In a school match against the MCC at Lords, he scored 144 not out in his first innings. When he went up to Trinity College, Cambridge, he got his Blues in football, cricket, tennis, real tennis and golf.

In 1914, he was playing first division football for Chelsea when war broke out. He volunteered, and saw action at Gallipoli, in the Middle East and on the Western Front. After the war he took a job in an engineering firm, but sport remained his passion. In 1919 he joined Manchester City and became widely regarded as the best midfielder and captain the club had ever known. Such was his talent that he was invited to join the British Olympic football squad for the 1920 Games, but he had already committed himself to play tennis.

Although knocked out early in the singles, he went on to win the men's doubles (with Oswald (Noel) Turnbull) and later in the day won silver in the mixed doubles with his partner Kitty Godfree.

The year 1921 was a busy one for Woosnam: he played the full season with Manchester City, becoming its captain midway through, captained the England amateur football team to a win over Wales, entered Wimbledon and was runner-up in the mixed doubles title, and headed for America as captain of the Davis Cup team.

It was during this visit to the States that Charlie Chaplin invited the team to stay at his Hollywood mansion. Chaplin first challenged Woosnam to a tennis match, and was soundly beaten. Next Chaplin challenged Woosnam to a game of table tennis. He was beaten again and, adding insult to injury, by a man using a butter knife instead of a bat! To crown it all, Woosnam playfully tossed him into his own swimming pool in the middle of his pre-dinner speech.

The following year Woosnam broke his leg in a match against Newcastle, which effectively put an end to his football career. Less mobile now, he nonetheless continued for the rest of his life to enjoy the other sports at which he once excelled. In 1940, he joined the chemical giant, ICI, eventually becoming a member of the board. Blond-haired, blue-eyed and with thighs like 'telegraph poles', Woosnam was described by the press as 'Captain Courageous', and 'The Admirable Crichton of sport'. Modest and self-

Max Woosnam (top left) and partner Oswald Turnbull in action against Ichiya Kumagae and Seiichiro Kashio of Japan. Great Britain won the match to claim the gold medal.

effacing, he never gave an interview in his life, but he was immensely popular in his time. Resolutely refusing to turn professional, Woosnam played sport because he loved it, not for fame or fortune.

Many have asked: Was he the greatest all-round sportsman ever? The answer is almost certainly, Yes.

Harold Abrahams
1924 Paris
Athletics, 100m

Abrahams' 100m victory at the 1924 Paris Olympics has become one of the best-known athletics performances of all time, after being immortalised in the Oscar-winning film *Chariots of Fire*. The film allowed itself more than a little artistic licence, since his great rival at the time, Eric Liddell, did not actually compete in the 100m final, his Presbyterian principles preventing him from competing on the Sabbath.

Abrahams had set his sights on winning a gold medal in the 100m, and Liddell's withdrawal must have been a great relief to him, since Liddell had set a record time of 9.7 seconds shortly before the Games. They did, however, meet in the 200m final, Liddell winning bronze and Abrahams finishing sixth. It was the only time they met on the track.

Harold Abrahams for many years dominated British long jump and sprint events and winning the Olympic 100m had become an obsession with him. Having competed unsuccessfully in the 1920 Olympics, he caused uproar in the establishment in 1924 by hiring a coach, Sam Mussabini. The relationship between them was one of the themes of *Chariots of Fire,* and the fierce reaction to this amateur being coached was put down to anti-Semitism. Mussabini gave this advice to Abrahams before the memorable race, 'Only think of two things, the report of the pistol and the tape. When you hear the one, just run like hell until you break the other.' Run like hell he did, setting an Olympic record of 10.6 seconds. He also won a silver medal in the 4x100m relay. A month before the Paris Games, he had set a new English long jump record of 7.36 metres, which stood for 32 years. There were no presentation ceremonies at the 1924 Games, and Abrahams received his medal in the post – after he had paid the excess postage on the package the French had failed to frank sufficiently.

A leg injury in 1925 cut short Abrahams' athletics career and he returned to the law, but he continued to distinguish himself as a writer, broadcaster and prominent figure in English amateur sports, as well as championing the development of Jewish representation in sport. His father had emigrated to England from Lithuania, and Abrahams admitted that his drive to succeed was spurred on by the growing anti-Semitism in England at the time.

Abrahams represented England and Northern Ireland on the International Amateur Athletic Federation (IAAF – later the International Association of Athletics Federations), was inducted into the International Jewish Sports Hall of Fame in 1981 and into the Veterans of the IAAF in 1948. He was awarded the CBE in 1957, as secretary of the National Parks Commission. He was the author of a number of books on Olympic history.

Harold Abrahams at the 1924 Games in Paris, where he broke the Olympic 100m record.

Jack Beresford

1924 Paris, 1932 Los Angeles and 1936 Berlin
Rowing, Single Sculls (1924), Coxless Fours (1932), Double Sculls (1936)

Jack Jr is acknowledged to be one of the greatest ever British oarsmen. Apart from his three Olympic gold medals, he won silver in the single sculls in 1920 in Antwerp and in the men's eights in 1928 in Amsterdam. His five medals in Olympic rowing is a record beaten only by Steve Redgrave's five gold medals in five separate games from 1984 to 2000, although Beresford might also have won a medal in the 1940 Games, had they not been cancelled because of the War.

Beresford was the son of a Polish furniture maker, Julius Wisniewski (he dropped his father's surname in early 1900), himself a notable oarsman and winner of an Olympic silver medal in 1912. At Bedford School, Beresford excelled at rowing and rugby. A leg wound received in the First World War precluded a career in rugby, but the rowing he did during recuperation set him on the path to a long and distinguished career as an oarsman. At Henley Royal Regatta Beresford won the Diamond Challenge Sculls four times, the Grand Challenge Cup (eights) twice, the Silver Goblets & Nickalls' Challenge Cup (pair) twice, the Stewards' Challenge Cup (coxless fours) and the Centenary Double Sculls. In the first Empire Games – now the Commonwealth Games – Beresford was runner-up in the men's single sculls.

In all, Beresford won the Amateur Sculling Championship a record eight times from 1920 to 1927. He said that 'the sweetest race I ever rowed in' was at the Berlin Games when he and Dick Southwood beat the Germans. The British had been warned by the German coach, Englishman Eric Phelps, that their boat was too light to stand a chance of winning. They duly had a heavier boat built, which went missing in transit to Berlin. At the last minute, it was located in a railway siding, and the pair won easily.

Beresford was a member of Thames Rowing Club at Putney in London, as captain in 1928–9 and as president from 1970 until his death in 1977. He became a steward of Henley Royal Regatta in 1946 and a member of the organising committee for the 1948 Olympic Games in London.

He was awarded the gold medal by the International Rowing Federation in 1947, the Olympic Diploma of Merit in 1949, and made a CBE in 1960. In 2005, in recognition of his achievements, English Heritage fixed a blue plaque on his former home in Chiswick, London.

Jack Beresford takes a breather during training in 1921. He went on to win the Olympic single sculls in 1924.

Eric Liddell
1924 Paris
Athletics, 400m

If not the greatest, Eric Liddell is certainly one of the best-known of Britain's sprinters. Universally popular, deeply devout and fast, very fast, Liddell's unique style of running has become familiar to millions after being portrayed in the famous feature film *Chariots of Fire*. Head thrown back, arms flailing and mouth agape, in his early days he ran 'more like a prancing circus pony than a world-class runner', as his Edinburgh University trainer, Tom McKerchar, said. This distinctive style was historically accurate (unlike various other scenes portrayed in the film).

Born in China to missionary parents, Liddell came to England with his elder brother when he was almost six years old, and both were enrolled in Eltham College in London.

In spite of being somewhat undernourished from his years in the inhospitable Great Plain of China, Liddell soon filled out and became an outstanding all-round sportsman. By the age of 15 he was captain of the cricket and rugby teams, as well as being one of the fastest runners. In his senior year he ran 100 yards in 10.2 seconds, a school record not to be broken for 80 years.

In 1921 he went up to Edinburgh University, and continued to excel. He played rugby for his university and was selected for the Scottish national team, playing in seven Five Nations matches.

Already dominant in athletics over 100m and 400m, he raced for the university and in 1923 won the Amateur Athletic Association (AAA) Championship 100m race in a British record time of 9.7 seconds (a record which stood for 35 years) and the 220 yards.

Eric Liddell, 'the Flying Scotsman', in characteristic style with head thrown back and arms flailing, breaks the tape to win the 400m final in 1924. 'I do not like to be beaten,' he would often repeat.

When the programme was announced for the 1924 Paris Games, and the 100m preliminary scheduled for a Sunday, Liddell declined to enter on religious grounds, opting instead to enter the AAA Championships again, in the 220 and 440 yards as a build-up to entering the Olympics in these distances. He came second in the 220 yards and won the 440 yards, and headed for Paris.

A few days after winning the bronze medal in the 200m, Liddell qualified for the 400m final – which was a classic. Spurred on by the pipes and drums of the Cameron Highlanders, he set off (in the outside lane and unable to see his opponents) at a blistering pace and won in a World, Olympic and European record time of 47.6 seconds. His time remained a world record for four years and a European record for 12 years. With stamina to spare, he celebrated his victory by attending a Tango Tea Dance on the Champs Elysées.

Liddell returned to university after the Olympics and graduated, but he continued to race. In 1925 at the Scottish AAA meeting he equalled his own Scottish championship record of 10 seconds in the 100 yards, won the 220 yards in 22.2 seconds and the 440 yards in 47.7 seconds, as well as being on the winning 4x400m relay team.

One scene portrayed in *Chariots of Fire* involved a race where Liddell was knocked down at the start of a 400m race. By the time he got to his feet, the field was 20m ahead, but, he went after them, caught them seconds before the finishing line, and collapsed as he crossed in first place. The story was true, although it took place in 1923 at a Triangular Contest and not, as the film depicted, in a Scotland–France meet. Nonetheless, it was hailed by *The Scotsman* newspaper as 'the greatest ever track performance ... ever seen'.

In spite of his passion for sport, it was his deep-rooted faith that was Liddell's driving force. At university and all through his gruelling athletics training, he continued to serve God, studying the Bible, evangelising and doing good works.

After a year of theological study, he was on his way back to China as a missionary to teach in the Anglo-Chinese College. Teaching science, religion and sports, he nonetheless found time to enter the Far Eastern Games, winning the 220 and 400m races.

By 1941, with the Chinese and Japanese long at war, life in China had become dangerous. But Liddell, now ordained and married, accepted a new position at a rural mission station in Shaochang where his brother was already serving, sending his pregnant wife and two daughters out of harm's way to Canada. In 1943 he was captured by the Japanese and interned. Under the brutal regime, Liddell retained his humour, his humility and humanity, and his faith, unstintingly giving succour to other unfortunate inmates.

In 1945, overworked and malnourished, he died of a brain tumour in the internment camp in Weifang. A fellow internee, Langdon Gilkey, later wrote, 'The entire camp, especially its youth, was stunned for days, so great was the vacuum that Eric's death had left'.

Liddell's last words were allegedly 'It's complete surrender'.

In 1990 his unmarked grave was discovered and a year later a monument of Scottish granite was erected in his honour in Weifang which bears the inscription:

'They shall mount up with wings as eagles; they shall run and not be weary'
(from the book of Isaiah)

David George Burghley (Marquess of Exeter)
1928 Amsterdam
Athletics, 400m Hurdles

'Leaping Lord' Burghley, Conservative politician, sports official and one of the world's greatest hurdlers, appeared in three Olympics: the first in 1924, where he was eliminated in the first round of the 100m hurdles, then in 1928 where he won a gold medal, and the third in 1932, where he won silver in the 4x400m relay.

A popular and dashing character, he caused a sensation in 1927 in his last year at Cambridge when he ran around the Great Court at Trinity College in the time it took the Trinity Clock to toll 12 o'clock. The event was portrayed in the film *Chariots of Fire*, but credited to Harold Abrahams. This naturally incensed Burghley, and he refused to see the film. His time of 43.10 was beaten in 2007 by 19-year-old student Sam Dobin, who shaved 0.33 of a second off it.

At one time Burghley was British record holder in all three hurdles events and the 1,500m relay. In the 400m hurdles, not only did he win a gold medal, but also set one world and seven British records, won five AAA titles and a gold medal at the 1930 Commonwealth Games, as well as a gold in the relay. His world record came in the 1927 AAA Championships, when he ran the 440 yards hurdles in 54.2 seconds.

Burghley set a somewhat more unusual record by racing round the promenade deck of the Queen Mary in 57 seconds, dressed in civvies. It was reported that he would place matchboxes on top of the hurdles and practice knocking them off with his lead foot without touching the hurdles.

Once, at a race meet in Antwerp, Burghley turned up at the wrong gate and was refused entry. He took a few paces backwards and, with bowler hat pulled down and attaché case in hand, leaped the four-foot gate and disappeared into the crowd.

Having entered Parliament in 1931, Burghley took leave of absence to compete in the Los Angeles Olympics. He was Member of Parliament for Peterborough from 1931 until 1943. He later served as President of the AAA for 40 years, President of the International Amateur Athletic Federation for 30 years and as a member of the International Olympic Committee for 48 years. He was also Chairman of the Organising Committee of the 1948 Olympics.

'Leaping Lord' Burghley on his way to winning the 400m hurdles in Amsterdam. For the race, his mother had provided him with silk shorts to prevent chafing of the legs.

Hugh (Jumbo) Edwards
1932 Los Angeles
Rowing, Coxless Pairs & Coxless Fours

In 1932 at the Los Angeles Olympics, Edwards became only the second man in history to win two rowing gold medals on the same day. He was scheduled to compete in the coxless pairs with Lewis Clive, a race they duly won in style in the morning. At the last minute one of the crew of the coxless fours was forced through illness to withdraw, and Edwards stepped in to replace him. A reshuffle in the boat saw John Badcock as stroke, Jack Beresford at two, Edwards at three and Roland George as bow. It proved a winning combination, and they stroked to a two-and-a-half length victory in the final that afternoon.

The start of Jumbo Edwards' rowing career was not auspicious. As a freshman at Christ Church, Oxford, he was selected for the 1926 Blue Boat, but collapsed during the race with what was later diagnosed as a hypertrophied heart. The following year his academic career took a nosedive as well, after he was rusticated for failing his exams. In spite of these setbacks, he got a job teaching and continued to row with the London Rowing Club. He returned to university in 1930 to complete his degree, hoping for a commission in the RAF. His winning streak in previous years led to a place in the Blue Boat. Not one to hide his light under a bushel, Edwards declared that he was 'incomparably the best oarsman in either crew'. They lost.

His heart condition notwithstanding, he went on to win the English eights and coxed fours at the Empire Games in Canada the same year.

While at Oxford he devoted much of his time to flying and kept his own light plane at university. In 1931 he obtained his commission in the RAF. During the war he served with Coastal Command, won the AFC in 1943 and the DFC in 1944, and his rowing experience stood him in good stead when his plane came down off Land's End in 1943. The only member of the crew to survive the crash, Edwards rowed his dinghy four miles to safety, dodging the mines.

In 1949 Edwards retired from the RAF as Group Captain and was invited back to Oxford to coach. Forthright and uncompromising, Edwards' relations with his colleagues were strained and he left in 1957, only to be brought back in 1959. His return sparked a rebellion and resignations in the squad, but Oxford won the Boat Race that year, and Edwards remains a legend at Oxford. One of Christ Church's coxless fours is named in his honour.

The winning crew of the coxless fours in 1932, Jumbo Edwards at number three.

Tommy Green
1932 Los Angeles
50km Road Walk

The 50km walk is a challenging enough event, but to win an Olympic gold medal walking it at the age of 38, having suffered rickets, been gassed and wounded numerous times, is a truly outstanding feat. In his day, Tommy Green was acknowledged to be the finest long-distance walker in the world, and he holds the distinction of being the first Olympic road-walking champion.

Green was born in 1894 and suffered from rickets as a child, and was unable to walk until he was five years old. He left school at 12, and in his late teens joined the 20th Hussars. He was invalided out after an accident, but joined up with the 3rd Hussars at the outbreak of the First World War. He served on the Western Front with the British Expeditionary Force, was wounded several times, gassed and invalided out again, with medals for bravery. Although the gas attack had damaged his lungs, Green remained a keen runner and boxer. In 1925 he was helping a blind friend train for the St Dunstan's London to Brighton walk, and was encouraged to take up the sport himself. The following year he won the first race he entered, from Worthing to Brighton, and there was no looking back. He went on to win the London to Brighton race four times, and the Manchester to Blackpool and Nottingham to Birmingham races six times. In 1930 he won the Milan 100km race, as well as the inaugural British 50km title.

Track walking had waned in popularity and been ruled out of the 1928 Amsterdam Games, but road walking had become fashionable and the British officials mounted efforts to have the sport introduced into the Olympics. They succeeded, and, with his impressive record, Green was an obvious choice for the first Olympic 50km road walk. He duly obliged by taking the gold medal in 4:50:10 – a slow time, but the conditions were said to be 'tropical'.

Having contested every major race every year since 1930 and now in his forties, Green set his sights on retaining his title at the 1936 Berlin Games. It was not to be, and he could only manage fourth place in the 50km Olympic selection race. In a fitting end to a glorious career, Green won his final competitive race at the age of 54, beating competitors half his age in the Poole to Wareham walk. He became a publican, but devoted much of his time to encouraging others to take up sport.

The indomitable Tommy Green, wearing number 12, in a road race in the UK.

Dickie Burnell and Bertie Bushnell
1948 London
Rowing, Double Sculls

Dickie Burnell and Bertie Bushnell only joined forces six weeks before the 1948 Olympics, but succeeded in winning the double sculls gold medal to a rousing ovation from the 30-deep crowd at Henley.

Like his father and fellow Olympic gold medallist, Burnell was educated at Eton and Magdalen College, Oxford. They are the only father and son in Olympic history to win rowing gold. Dickie rowed in the Oxford boat in 1939, went to war and was decorated for bravery.

In 1948, with Burnell as stroke and Bushnell at bow, they lost the first round of the double sculls at Henley to France, but won the repêchage and went on to win the gold medal. The first-round loss was apparently a deliberate ploy to avoid meeting their chief rivals, Denmark, until the final. The strategy certainly worked.

In later life Burnell commented on the celebrations of his day compared to those of more recent times, saying, 'After the racing, the oarsmen had a dinner, threw bread rolls at each other and then went home'. According to Bushnell, however, the dinner degenerated into a brawl with the Americans, who took exception to the poor standard of food.

Burnell took a bronze medal in the eights at the Commonwealth Games of 1950, and won the Double Sculls Challenge Cup in 1951. He

Burnell and Bushnell stand proudly to attention for the National Anthem after winning their gold medal in the double sculls in 1948.

was *The Times* rowing correspondent from 1946 to 1967, and became a leading historian of the sport, one of his best-known works being *The Complete Sculler*.

Bushnell and Burnell made an unlikely pair in the double sculls, coming as they did from different backgrounds and being of dramatically different stature. Bushnell's family owned a boatyard at Wargrave, with a branch at Henley. When young Bertie showed great promise as an oarsman, his father apprenticed him as a marine engineer rather than taking him into the family firm, thus enabling him to keep his amateur status. The Eton and Oxford blue, Burnell, topped six foot four, Bushnell a mere five foot nine and several stone lighter. But, having been thrown together only weeks before the event and despite some initial friction, they won the gold medal to the delight of the crowd.

Bushnell had toured South Africa the winter before the Olympics, maintaining an unbeaten record. During the Games, he made friends with Jack Kelly, whose family had come over from Philadelphia. Jack rowed in the single sculls, winning a bronze medal, but it was his sister,

Grace, who was the main attraction – particularly for Bushnell, who succeeded where others had failed in taking 'Little Gracie' out on a date. Eighteen months later, he received a postcard from her saying she had enrolled in dance school, her springboard to Hollywood.

Bushnell retired from rowing in 1951 to join the family firm. He later set up a successful river-cruise hire company on the Thames, pioneering the development of recirculative 'pump-out' lavatories, which earned him the affectionate nickname 'Recirc Bert'. He died in 2010.

Harry Llewellyn
1952 Helsinki
Equestrian, Team Jumping

Queen Elizabeth II had just acceded to the throne when the debonair aristocrat Sir Harry Llewellyn and his gelding, Foxhunter, went clear in the final round of the show jumping at Helsinki to give Britain its only gold medal of the Games. The team had had indifferent scores in the preliminary rounds and were lying sixth. On the final morning, Llewellyn himself had three fences down, a refusal and time penalties, and at midday was dejectedly blaming himself for the team's poor performance overall. He refused lunch and lay down for an hour's sleep (while the horse also snoozed). When he returned to the ring, refreshed and focused, he rode a flawless clear round and the gold medal was theirs. Llewellyn and Foxhunter were hailed as heroes. The new Queen and her Prime Minister, Churchill, sent congratulatory telegrams. Llewellyn was embarrassed by the adulation and

media attention, and throughout his life sought to play it down, modestly emphasising that, though the captain, he had clocked up the most faults and was undeserving of all the praise.

The son of the Welsh colliery owner and first Baronet, Sir David Llewellyn, Harry went to Oundle and then up to Cambridge. Though a keen sportsman, as a youth his riding was limited to a little hunting and the odd point-to-point. His enthusiasm for the latter was somewhat dampened by the fact that his father, an inveterate gambler, would wager huge sums on his winning. He did, however, go on to become a successful amateur steeplechase jockey, winning 60 races under National Hunt rules and coming second and fourth in the Grand National in 1936 and 1937 respectively. He and Foxhunter took part in the 1948 Olympics, winning the bronze medal.

At the outbreak of war in 1939, Llewellyn took a commission in the Warwickshire Yeomanry, eventually rising to Lieutenant Colonel. He was senior liaison officer to General Montgomery, was mentioned in despatches, and was awarded the American Legion of Merit and, in 1944, the OBE.

Although his partnership with Foxhunter lasted a mere five years, between them they succeeded in winning 78 international competitions, including three King George V Gold Cups, show jumping's most prestigious trophy. Llewellyn was known for his easy-going manner, charm and diplomacy, and Foxhunter too appears to have had a sense of humour: at the 1949 Nations Cup, as the prizes were awarded by a Swiss general's wife, the horse caused hilarity in the crowd by calmly munching the floral decoration of her hat.

Llewellyn was married to the daughter of the 5th Baron de Saumarez, and their sons, Dai and Roddy, were much in the public eye during the 1960s and '70s owing to their romantic entanglements – Dai with Tessa Dahl and Beatrice Welles and Roddy with Princess Margaret, who was said to have been much in love with him.

On retirement from competition, Llewellyn continued his involvement in show jumping, becoming chef d'équipe of the British team, notably during the Mexico Games of 1968, and as Chairman and then Honorary Vice-President of the British Show Jumping Association (BSJA).

Llewellyn and Foxhunter remain one of the best-loved and best-remembered partnerships. When Llewellyn died in 1999, the Chief Executive of the BSJA said of him, 'His was an era of show jumping that to this day we aspire to emulate. His knowledge and experience were second to none.' His ashes were scattered over the grave of his beloved mount.

A caricature of Sir Harry Llewellyn by Dorrien.

Chris Brasher
1956 Melbourne
Athletics, 3,000m Steeplechase

Chris Brasher will be remembered for many things other than his gold medal and his part in breaking the four-minute mile. In addition to these notable achievements, he was a journalist, broadcaster, mountaineer, orienteer, businessman and founder of the London Marathon.

Born in Guyana and educated at Rugby and Cambridge, Brasher's athletics career began with middle-distance running, but in 1951 he turned to steeplechasing. In spite of finishing eleventh in the Olympic qualifier final, Brasher made the British team. In 1954, at Iffley Road, Oxford, he secured his place in athletics annals as a contributor in Roger Bannister becoming the first man to run the mile in under four minutes. Brasher acted as a pacemaker for Bannister early in the race, making way for Christopher Chataway in a similar role. Roger Bannister broke the tape in 3:59.4.

At Melbourne in 1956, Brasher was not expected to win and, even after finishing with a personal best, Olympic and British record time of 8:41.2, he was still not sure that he had won. Although he was way ahead of the field, an objection was lodged and it was three agonising hours before the result was confirmed. In great relief, he and his friends celebrated until late into the evening, and when he came to receive his medal the next day he was, as he said, 'totally blotto, with an asinine grin on my face'.

Leaving his job with Mobil Oil after Melbourne, Brasher joined *The Observer* as Sports Editor. In 1961, he joined the BBC, starting as a reporter and rising to become Head of General Features.

In 1979 he went to New York to run the marathon, and was so impressed by the egalitarianism of the event he determined London should have its own marathon. By 1981 he had organised it. His highest hopes were fulfilled when more than 7,000 runners assembled in Greenwich Park, most of them making it to the finish at Buckingham Palace, and Brasher himself completing in under three hours. Within a few years, it had become the

Chris Brasher, followed by Roger Bannister, during the race in 1954 which saw Bannister break the 4-minute mile.

biggest annual marathon in the world, a testament to his popularity and ability.

He is known also as the father of orienteering. With John Disley he founded the Southern Navigators Orienteering Club, sowing the seeds of enthusiasm in many generations. With the increased interest in running in the 1970s and 1980s, Brasher set up his own sportswear shop (eventually known as the Sweatshop), where he sold, among other things, a lightweight shoe of his own design. He was awarded the CBE in 1996 and died in 2003.

Anita Lonsbrough
1960 Rome
Swimming, 200m Breaststroke

At the age of 19, Huddersfield's 'Princess of the Pool' achieved the first of Britain's only two gold medals in Rome in a gripping 200m breaststroke final, when she beat the West German favourite by half a second in an Olympic and world record time of 2:49.5. Bouts of gastroenteritis, flu and shingles in the run-up to the Games had made her participation doubtful, but by August she had struggled back to fitness. As she lined up for the final race, a bug in the water below her was only a slight distraction for the girl who had had to fish the cockroaches out of the pool in Huddersfield before training. It turned out to be one of swimming's most closely fought races, bringing the crowd and the commentators to the edge of their seats as Lonsbrough and the German, Wiltrud Urselmann, exchanged the lead twice in the closing few metres. It was Britain's last women's swimming gold medal for 48 years, until Rebecca Adlington's achievements at the 2008 Games.

Anita Lonsbrough learned to swim in India, where her Coldstream Guards father was stationed. Settling in Yorkshire in her teens, she began to train in earnest. In 1958 she broke through to the top ranks by winning her first gold medal in the Empire Games in Cardiff. The following year she was voted Amateur Swimming Association's swimmer of the year.

'The Princess of the Pool' won the first of Britain's two gold medals in Rome.

In the years between 1958 and 1962 Lonsbrough broke five world records and won seven international gold medals. At one time she held the Olympic, Empire and European titles simultaneously. She became the first female BBC Sports Personality of the Year in 1962 and in 1963 was awarded the MBE.

In 1964 she was again part of the British Olympic team, and was given the honour of bearing the Union Jack in the opening ceremony, marking yet another record by being the first woman to do so at a Summer Games. Once more afflicted with illness she nonetheless competed and, although she won no medals, she did meet her future husband, Hugh Porter, an outstanding cyclist, Commonwealth gold medallist, and World Professional 5,000m Cycling Champion. In November 1964 Lonsbrough announced her retirement and in 1965 married Hugh.

The couple moved to Wolverhampton and embarked on long and successful careers in broadcasting, she becoming first the *Sunday* then *The Daily Telegraph*'s swimming correspondent, and he a BBC sports commentator.

Robin Dixon and Tony Nash
1964 Innsbruck
2-man Bobsleigh

The story of the Nash-Dixon route to Olympic gold sounds like a tall one, featuring as it does Lord Lucan, tons of imported snow, a broken sled, a selfless Italian and a victorious nation with no bobsleigh run of its own.

The names of Nash and Dixon are inextricably linked – like horse and carriage they go together. And just as firmly wedded to their historic, one-and-only British bobsleigh gold medal is the name of Eugenio Monti, without whom there would have been no British victory.

The Hon. Robin Dixon came to the sport after a chance meeting with his cousin, Lord Lucan, in St Moritz in 1957. Lucan, aware of Dixon's all-round sporting ability and particularly his sprinting, persuaded Dixon to have a go in the four-man bob. He 'quite enjoyed' it and before long had become part of the British team. Meanwhile, Tony Nash was approaching international sledding from an equally unlikely direction. Although a director in his family's engineering firm which was instrumental in the development of the British bobsleigh, Nash was entirely self-taught, extremely short-sighted and had no driving experience.

By 1958 the pair had met on the four-man team, and in 1960 decided to form a two-man partnership with Nash as pilot and Dixon as brakeman. They entered the 1961 World Championship and came sixth. With no funding forthcoming, an Olympic medal seemed unlikely. Then, thanks to the gregarious Nash's friendship with the Italian team, the duo were invited to join them in training at Cervino.

By 1964 they were reckoned to be in with a chance of a medal in Innsbruck – if there was enough ice. In the nick of time, 30,000 soldiers managed to shovel in sufficient snow and British confidence rose. Their first run was fast and they were in second place when disaster struck. The bolt attaching the runners to the shell had snapped. When Monti, the Italian sledding star, heard of this he said, 'Get an Englishman and a spanner ... and they can have my bolt'. The bolt from the Italian sled was fitted, and the British won by 12/100ths of a second.

Monti's generosity had also extended to repairing Canada's damaged sled (enabling them to win the four-man bob), while he himself had to settle for bronze in both events. His selflessness earned him the first Pierre de Coubertin award for fair play. Though criticised by many a disappointed Italian, Monti said, 'Nash didn't win because I gave him the bolt. He won because he had the fastest run.' To the rest of the world he was a hero and the embodiment of Olympic sportsmanship, and deservedly won gold medals in the two- and four-man events at the next Olympics.

Nash and Dixon were each awarded the MBE and went on to win the world title in 1964 and 1965. There is a turn at the St Moritz course named after the pair.

Since 1987 Dixon has been the President of the British Bobsleigh Association. He was awarded the CBE in 1993 for services to Northern Ireland and to industry. He succeeded his father as Lord Glentoran in 1998. He has also been Shadow Minister for Northern Ireland, for Sport and for Environment, Food and Rural Affairs, and was the Conservative Shadow Minister for the Olympics in the House of Lords.

Tony Nash (pilot) and Robin Dixon on their way to the gold medal in Innsbruck – Britain's first gold medal at the Winter Olympics in 12 years.

Mary Rand
1964 Tokyo
Athletics, Long Jump

'Mary was the most gifted athlete I ever saw. She was as good as athletes get, there has never been anything like her since. And I don't believe there ever will be.' So said Ann Packer, friend, teammate and roommate at the 1964 Games. It was an opinion shared by a great many people, for Mary Rand became the first British woman to win a gold medal in a track and field event. Blonde, beautiful and charismatic, the 'Golden Girl' of athletics spent her career smashing records and turning men's heads. In Tokyo she beat the Olympic record with all of her seven jumps and took the gold medal with a massive distance of 6.76m.

Born in Somerset in 1940, the schoolgirl Mary Bignal could outrun, outjump and outswim her contemporaries of either sex. When she was 16 she was offered an athletics scholarship at Millfield School, where her immense talent was nurtured. She won the All-England schools title, and once when she joined the British Olympic squad in training, she outjumped the nation's best jumpers.

At 19 she was already an international long jumper, high jumper and hurdler. She was never beaten in the long jump between 1958 and 1960. She had begun an affair with a fellow-student, Jimmy Burakamkovit, and when she defied the headmaster's edict to end it, was expelled from Millfield. She and Jimmy became engaged, but it lasted only until she met the Dutch athlete Eef Kamerbeek. And that romance lasted only until she was introduced to the rower Sidney Rand in 1961. Three days after meeting him they became engaged, and were married within five weeks.

Selected for the British squad at the 1960 Rome Olympics, hopes were high that she would return with at least one medal. But although she led after the qualifying round with a British record jump of 6.33m, nerves got the better of her and she finished only ninth. She also finished fourth in the 80m hurdles.

It was all very different when she went to Tokyo. In the qualifying rounds of the long jump she set an Olympic record of 6.52m, a British record with her first jump of the final, and in the fifth round on a soggy track and with a strong headwind broke the world record. She also won a silver medal in the women's modern pentathlon (which might have been another

Mary Rand in action at the Tokyo Games in 1964, as she smashes the world long jump record.

gold medal had the real sex of the winner, Irina Press, been discovered sooner) and a bronze in the 4x100m relay. Returning home triumphant, she was voted BBC Sports Personality of the Year and awarded the MBE. She was invited to lunch at Buckingham Palace and the Queen asked her to show the young Prince Andrew just how far the winning leap was. As she paced it out on the floor, the Prince exclaimed, 'Nobody could jump *that* far!' In 1966 she won a gold medal at the Commonwealth Games and in 1968 retired.

Her marriage to Sid Rand ended after five years and there was no shortage of suitors for Mary; Mick Jagger once described her as his dream date. But in 1968 she married another athlete, Bill Toomey, the Olympic decathlon gold medallist. That marriage lasted 22 years, after which she married an American, John Reese, with whom she now lives in California.

Back home in Wells, her winning long jump is marked out on the pavement of the market square, and in January 2012 she was granted the freedom of the city. She remains the only British woman to hold a long jump world record.

Mary Rand's world record distance of 6.76m is marked out in her home town of Wells, Somerset.

Lynn Davies
1964 Tokyo
Athletics, Long Jump

'Lynn the Leap', as Davies was affectionately known to his Welsh compatriots, was a talented athlete. In 1964, in howling wind and driving rain, competing against two men who had regularly jumped a great deal further than him and not fancied to win anything, Davies made the jump of his life and with a distance of 8.07m took the gold medal. On his return home, ecstatic crowds were there to meet him, bringing Cardiff to a standstill.

Davies began his sporting career as a footballer, was a fine sprinter and triple jumper, but truly made his name as an outstanding long jumper, thanks in large part to the encouragement of Ron Pickering, coach and BBC commentator.

Pickering asked him if he 'wanted to be greatest athlete Wales had ever produced and whether he was prepared to work harder than any other athlete had ever worked?' His answer was Yes, and he is still the only Welshman to

Lynn Davies makes the leap of his life in the pouring rain in Tokyo.

win an individual Olympic Athletics gold medal.

He made his international debut in 1961 at the European Championships, and the following year at the Commonwealth Games broke the British record. In 1964 he created two new Commonwealth records, and made yet another with his gold-medal winning Olympic leap. At Tokyo he also competed in the 100m and 4x100m relay, reaching the final.

In 1966 Davies became the first athlete to hold the European, Commonwealth and Olympic titles. He continued to improve on the Commonwealth record in 1968, setting a record of 8.23m, which stood for 33 years. Returning to the Olympics that year he was denied the gold medal by Bob Beamon's legendary leap of 8.9m – a jump which remains an Olympic record was and so huge that it was beyond the equipment's range and had to be measured by hand. Davies attended his third Olympics in 1972, but missed out on the medals again.

Ranked as one of Britain's greatest athletes, in 1967 Davies was made an MBE, and in 2006 a CBE. Following his retirement as an athlete in 1973 he was appointed technical director of Canadian Track and Field Association, and on returning to the UK became team manager of the British athletics team.

He was Senior Lecturer in physical education at the University of Wales Institute, Cardiff (UWIC), and a member of the Sports Council for Wales for two terms. Davies played a key role in London's successful 2012 Olympic bid and continues to be involved in the organisation of the event. A consultant and broadcaster for the BBC, he is currently President of UK Athletics, and one of the sport's finest ambassadors.

Jane Bullen (Holderness-Roddam)
Mexico City 1968
Equestrian 3-Day Event Team Competition

Jane Holderness-Roddam (née Bullen) is a lady of exceptional charm, energy and determination, the first woman to compete in an Olympic 3-day equestrian event and the first British woman to win a gold medal. She also has the curious distinction of having been Tatum O'Neal's double in the film *International Velvet*. She was chosen as an official Olympic torchbearer for the 2012 Games.

Riding her own diminutive horse Our Nobby (only an inch or so from being a pony), her name is unfairly not registered in many of the record books alongside those of her Olympic team mates, Derek Allhusen, Ben Jones and Richard Meade. Only the three top scores count in IOC records, which fails to recognise her contribution to their success. In the testing altitude of Mexico City, the British team was by far the fittest of the equestrian entrants, thanks largely to their coach Bertie Hill's preparations. The '68 Games were a highly politicised event, made infamous by the shooting of protesters by the Mexican army 10

Jane Bullen, the only woman among the 12 medallists (there's an American missing from the left of the picture). The British contingent comprises, from left to right, Ben Jones, Jane Bullen, Richard Meade and Major Derek Allhusen.

days before the start and the Black Power salute by two American athletes from the podium. But the British team's focus did not waver. Later Derek Allhusen was awarded the MBE, but declined to accept it on the grounds that his teammates were not given the same honour.

Jane herself was already as fit as a flea, and was selected for the team on the strength of a fine win at Badminton that year (having been fifth the previous year) – again on Our Nobby. She went on to win a gold medal at the European Championships at Burghley in 1977.

One of six children, Jane grew up with horses. Her parents had founded the Catherston Stud and bred mostly Welsh ponies. Her mother Anne Bullen was a famous illustrator of children's books and two of her siblings have also achieved distinction in the equestrian world – Jennie (Loriston-Clarke) and Michael between them attended seven Olympic Games.

A mark of her guts and dedication is the fact that despite suffering since childhood with a painful condition of the feet – the result, she says, of wearing too many of her siblings' wellies, but more likely a genetic anomaly – she still managed a successful career in nursing (as an SRN and constantly on her feet) and in equestrianism. She also ran the London Marathon. Recognising that the young nurse had a chance to achieve Olympic gold, the Middlesex Hospital re-arranged her shifts to allow for training, and gave her leave of absence to compete in Mexico. By the time she set off for the Games she had been dubbed 'the galloping nurse' by the press.

A Lady-in-Waiting to the Princess Royal, a Lieutenant of the Royal Victorian Order and holder of the Queen's Award for Equestrianism, she was awarded the CBE in 2004. Practical and unassuming, she makes little of her tireless work for charity, and the list of her achievements in and for equestrianism is far too long to list in this small space – although skydiving at the age of 60 to raise money for Riding for the Disabled certainly deserves a mention.

Not only is she the author of 27 books on horses and equestrianism, she was for many years Chair of Riding for the Disabled, British Eventing, the British Equestrian Federation, President of the British Equestrian Trade Association, Patron of the Side Saddle Association and an FEI technical delegate and judge: all this while running the highly successful West Kington Stud in north Wiltshire with her husband Tim. There they breed competition horses, run training courses and workshops, and have a state-of-the-art sperm bank. One focus of the stud – and of much of Jane's life – is to improve the welfare of horses and ponies.

As the British Horse Society Chairman said on presenting the Queen's Award, 'It is difficult to think of any other equestrian who, having first achieved high acclaim as a competitor, has gone on to earn such high distinction by energetically promoting the interests of others within the sport'.

Jane Holderness-Roddam carried the Olympic torch through Shurdington, Gloucestershire, in May 2012.

Chris Finnegan
1968 Mexico City
Boxing, Middleweight

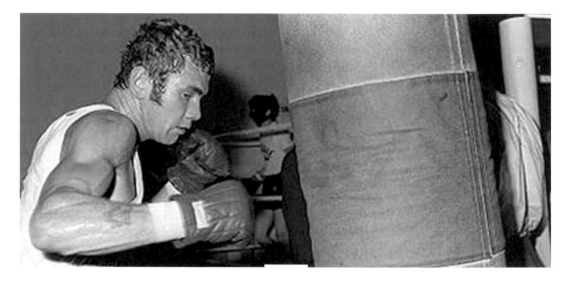

Chris Finnegan works out in preparation for the 1968 Games.

Hard drinking, straight talking and immensely brave, Chris Finnegan was one of Britain's most popular and colourful boxers. His win at the 1968 Games gave Britain its only Olympic boxing gold medal between 1956 and 2000, and its first middleweight gold since 1924.

In his early days, the frequently out-of-work Anglo-Irish brickie Finnegan was a bruiser in and out of the ring, often in trouble with the law and fond of his Guinness. He and his younger brother Kevin, who became European and British middleweight champion, sparred with each other mercilessly, and their training sessions were legendary battles. In 1965, with his long reach and southpaw stance, the elder Finnegan became Amateur Boxing Association (ABA) middleweight champion, and looked to be in line for inclusion in the British squad for Mexico City. But an eye injury prevented him from winning the 1967 ABA championships, making his place uncertain. Finnegan in his disappointment embarked on a two-week drinking binge. Hauled back on the straight and narrow and offered a place in the Olympic team, he faced another setback when he was summonsed to appear in court for non-payment of his National Insurance stamp. The presiding magistrate, however, gave him a reprieve and wished him luck. When Finnegan returned victorious, his £70 debt to the government was paid by boxing promoter Harry Levene.

In Mexico City, Finnegan survived two standing counts in the semi-final and went on to win the final against the Russian, Aleksei Kiselyov, by a 3-2 verdict. His wife Cheryl was not present for his finest hour, having elected to stay in England in the (delusive) expectation of winning a 'trip of a lifetime' competition staged by Golden Wonder crisps. When Finnegan stepped out of the ring to be interviewed, he was connected by satellite to Cheryl, knee-deep in crisp packets, who said, 'You 'aven't fucking gone and done it, 'ave you?' To which he replied, 'Yes, old lady, I fucking, fucking 'ave!'

The final was a close one, but Finnegan found his troubles just beginning when asked afterwards to provide a urine sample for drugs testing. 'Now if there's one thing I've never been able to do, it's have a piss while someone's watching me.' The Olympic officials trailed after him as he had dinner, copious pints of beer and water, until in the early hours of the morning he finally shouted, 'Who wants some piss?' The tests were negative, of course.

Finnegan returned to England a hero, was awarded the MBE and immediately turned professional. Of his 37 professional contests, he won 29, lost seven and drew one.

In 1971, he moved up to the light-heavyweight division and a meeting with American legend Bob Foster was scheduled for the following year.

Finnegan was knocked out in the 14th round of a gruelling fight, but the bout was regarded as a classic and named Fight of the Year by *The Ring* magazine. Finnegan likened Foster's punch to 'being hit with a scaffolding pole with a boxing glove on the end of it'.

He lost again that year when defending his European title, but retained his British and Commonwealth titles. Then he met the up-and-coming young Liverpudlian, John Conteh. In 1973 he lost the British, European and Commonwealth title fight to Conteh after 15 rounds, and failed to regain it in the rematch the next year.

In 1975, Conteh relinquished the title to move to world honours, and Finnegan met 'Gypsy' Johnny Frankham for the vacant British title. Although he lost on points after 15 rounds, he won the rematch later the same year and fittingly retired as the title-holder. He always wore a Union Flag and a Shamrock on his boxing trunks to show his joint heritage.

Shortly before the 2008 Olympics, he commented with typically wry humour on the British team's preparations for coping with Beijing's altitude: 'I was up and down a 30-rung ladder all day with piles of bricks on both my flippin' shoulders. That was the only bloody altitude training I did, mate.'

On retirement, the ebullient Finnegan became a publican – alas, an unsuccessful one. He described his life after boxing as being spent 'ducking and diving'. He found time, however, to write his autobiography, *Finnegan: Self-Portrait of a Fighting Man*.

He died in 2008 of pneumonia, only months after the death of his brother Kevin.

David Hemery
1968 Mexico City
Athletics, 400m Hurdles

David Hemery's dream of being Olympic champion came true in Mexico City with a blistering, record-breaking run which was watched in the small hours by millions of jubilant Britons. As he crossed the line in a world record time of 48.12, it was a moment when, as he put it, his body and soul were in alignment. His victory gave Britain its only track and field gold medal of the Games.

As Hemery stormed ahead of the field to take the tape, the BBC commentator, David Coleman, hysterically screamed, 'And it's David Hemery in the lead for Great Britain. It's Hemery . . . it's Hemery . . . it's HEMERY! Hemery takes the gold, Hennige, of West Germany, the silver, and who cares who's third? It doesn't matter.' A typical 'Colemanball', since the bronze medal was taken by another Briton, John Sherwood. Hemery's performance earned him the accolade of BBC's Sports Personality of the Year.

Having won the European Championship in 1969, injury kept Hemery off the track for some time, but in 1972 he went to Munich to defend his title. He could only manage third place, but won a silver medal in the 4x400m relay.

On retirement in 1973, Hemery returned to America, where he had been brought up, to coach, though he returned frequently to England on coaching assignments and for a time taught at Millfield School. He received the CBE in 1969 and was elected the first president of UK Athletics in 1998. He is currently the Vice Chairman of the British Olympic Association, has been heavily involved with the preparation for the 2012 Games, and is a leading figure behind the '21st Century Legacy' project. In 2011 he became the first Briton to be awarded the European Olympic Committees' Laurel Award for outstanding sporting merit and services to sport.

To add to his clutch of Olympic and European medals, Hemery won the first British Superstars competition in 1973, and again in 1976.

David Hemery hurdling to victory in Mexico City in 1968.

Rodney Pattisson
1968 Mexico City and 1972 Munich
Sailing, Flying Dutchman Class

Rodney Pattisson was the first Scot to win an Olympic gold medal in sailing, and until Ben Ainslie's three gold medals in successive Games, he was Britain's most successful Olympic yachtsman with two golds and a silver. He is still considered by many to be one of the greatest Scottish sportsmen, up there with Eric Liddell, Chris Hoy and David Wilkie.

The Flying Dutchman is a two-man racing dinghy, and the significance of Pattisson's three medals is that he won each of them with a different crew. With Iain MacDonald Smith, he won the 1968 World and European Championships, before setting off for Mexico. After meticulous preparation, hard training, and three months practice in the waters off Mexico they won five of their seven races in the fancifully-named *Superdocious* – a shortening of its original *Supercalifragilisticexpialidocious*, which was rather too long to fit on the 20-foot vessel – and beat the opposition by one of the biggest winning margins ever recorded.

In the years following, Pattisson dominated the class, winning the World Championships in 1969, '70 and '71, and was well prepared for his second Games. In 1972, with Christopher Davies, he was on the podium again in the Port of Kiel to receive his medal, the first Scot to win two golds.

For his achievements Pattisson was selected as flag-bearer at the opening ceremony of the 1976 Montreal Olympics. As crew, he had Justin Brooke Houghton, with whom he had won his third World Championship, but they were beaten into second place by the West Germans.

Pattisson attended Pangbourne College, the public school largely geared to preparing boys to be naval officers. At 17, he won the world cadet title, with his brother crewing, and on leaving school followed the College's tradition by joining the Royal Navy. When he resigned his commission in 1968 to concentrate full-time on sailing, he was a submarine lieutenant, and in 1969 was awarded the MBE. Although he took no further part in the Olympics after Montreal, in spite of coming close to making the team in 1984, Pattisson co-skippered Peter de Savary's *Victory 83* in the 1983 America's Cup. His passion for the sport extended beyond the Flying Dutchman Class in which he was pre-eminent, and included the quarter-ton (in which he was world champion), and 12-metre Classes.

Through rigorous attention to detail, supreme fitness and outstanding ability, his success has made Pattisson a yachtsman of whom Scotland and Britain are justifiably proud.

Rodney Pattisson at the helm during the 1972 Munich Games.

Mary Peters
1972 Munich
Modern Pentathlon

Mary Peters was 33 years old when she went to Munich in 1972 filled with determination to win a gold medal at her third Olympic attempt in the pentathlon. For two gruelling days she battled it out with the favourite, West Germany's Heide Rosendahl. By the end of the first day, Peters had set personal bests in the hurdles, shot putt and high jump and was in the lead. The following day her long jump distance fell short of Rosendahl's 6.83m and success rested on the 200m, which was Rosendahl's strongest event. Peters gave it everything she had, but saw her rival drawing ahead as the line approached. The screams of the sell-out crowd as she crossed the line ten metres behind Rosendahl subsided to an expectant hush.

Agonising minutes passed as the scores were calculated. Then a roar went up as it was announced that Peters had won by a mere ten points, with a world and Olympic record score of 4,801 points.

Peters' path to glory had not been easy. Though a world-class athlete and a tireless worker, she admitted to having an attitude problem and to being 'a bit afraid of success'. Born in Merseyside, she was brought up in Northern Ireland and always declared herself an Ulsterwoman. The Troubles in her adopted country formed a backdrop to her entire career. Bullied at school and devastated when her mother died and her father married their housekeeper, she channelled her energies into athletics. She represented Northern Ireland at every Commonwealth

Games from 1958 to 1974 and Great Britain internationally from 1961 to 1974. At the Commonwealth Games in 1970 she won gold medals in the shot putt and pentathlon, and in the pentathlon in 1974.

But in 1972 the Troubles were at their height, her father had moved to Australia and she faced huge difficulties with training – commuting through the bombed streets of Belfast to a heavily fortified gym and an inferior track. A gold

Mary Peters flies off the starting blocks in the 200m sprint, the last discipline of the pentathlon, in 1972.

medal looked improbable, but six weeks before the Games she was offered a scholarship to train in America. Her mental attitude hardened from a desire to do well and be admired into a steely determination to win. And what a success, what an overwhelmingly popular success! As she was being interviewed by Chris Brasher after receiving the gold medal, from behind a screen stepped her father, whom she had not seen for two years. It was the icing on the cake for Peters.

Two days later came the terrorist attack on the Israeli quarters in the Olympic Village. Six months later her coach, Buster McShane, was killed in a car crash. Plunged from the heights to the depths, Mary's spirit and goodness nonetheless survived.

Now in her 70s, she remains committed to sport and to Northern Ireland, and to helping others. Since retiring from athletics she has dedicated herself to charitable and community causes.

She was awarded the MBE in 1973, the CBE in 1990, was made a Dame Commander of the British Empire in 2000 and in 2009 was appointed Lord Lieutenant of Belfast. The Mary Peters Trust, which helps young sportsmen and -women of Northern Ireland to achieve their dreams, has set its sights firmly on the 2012 Games and nurturing native talent.

A woman of humility and humour, guts and graciousness, Mary Peters is a true sporting hero and an inspiration to millions.

John Curry
1976 Innsbruck
Figure Skating

Known as 'the Nureyev of the ice', John Curry was Britain's first Olympic skating gold medallist, giving one of the most memorable performances in skating history at the Winter Games in 1976.

As a child, he had wanted to be a ballet dancer, but his stern father disapproved so at the age of seven he took up skating. Such was his talent and dedication that it was only a year before he won his first competition. In 1967 he won the British Junior Championship, and went on to win the British Seniors four times from 1972 to 1975, as well as winning both the World and European Championships in 1976.

After his father died when he was 16, having seen his son skate only twice, Curry moved to London to start the previously forbidden ballet lessons. In 1972 he attended the Olympics in Munich and, although he came nowhere near the medals, succeeded in securing the sponsorship he badly needed to finance his career. With the backing of American millionaire Ed Moseler, Curry went to the United States and trained under the renowned Carlo Fassi in Colorado.

At the peak of his career in 1976, as European, World and Olympic Champion, he turned professional, founded a successful ice dance company, was voted BBC Sports Personality of the Year and was awarded the OBE.

Curry had come out publicly as gay just prior to the Olympics, a brave move given the prevailing attitude to homosexuality. His sexuality, and possibly his troubled relationship with his father, had made him notoriously difficult to work with and highly critical of himself and others. At the post-Sports Personality of the Year award dinner, he was mocked for being a 'fairy', leading to a worsening of his already poor relationship with the press.

In 1987 Curry was diagnosed as HIV-positive. When he developed full-blown Aids in 1990 he returned to England to live with his mother. One of his earlier lovers, the actor Alan Bates, returned to look after him in his final days. According to Bates, Curry died in his arms. He was only 44 years old.

Curry's influence on the sport was profound. With his balletic style he transformed skating, turning it into an art form with a combination of athleticism, technique and creative imagination.

John Curry in characteristically artistic pose in 1976.

Sebastian Coe (Baron Coe of Ranmore)
1980 Moscow and 1984 Los Angeles
Athletics, 1,500m

Sebastian Coe is the only man to have successfully defended the Olympic 1,500m title and is possibly the greatest middle-distance runner ever. He dominated international athletics for more than a decade, along with his long-time rival Steve Ovett. In all, he set 12 world records during his career (more than any other Briton), and won two Olympic gold medals and two silvers.

Coe showed early signs of his extraordinary ability, winning the British Youth and Junior 1,500m titles at the age of 16 in 1973. He followed this by setting a new British 800m indoor record of 1:47.6 in 1977, breaking that record twice within a month, and a third time shortly after. In an astonishing show of brilliance, over six weeks in July and August of 1979, he set new world records for the 800m, 1,500m, and 1 mile. In 1980, he became the world record holder at 1,000m, in 1981 broke his own records again at 800m and 1,000m, and twice improved the mile time. This extraordinary success continued in 1982, when he contributed a world record time of 1:44.01 to the 4x800m relay, as well as setting new indoor records at 800m and 1,000m. His 800m record of 1:41.73 has only been beaten once, by Wilson Kipketer of Denmark in 1997; it still stands as a British record.

The duel between Coe and Ovett, with their contrasting backgrounds and personalities – Coe the suave, media-conscious runner from London and Ovett the 'bad boy' of athletics who antagonised the press – caught the public imagination and became one of the most famous rivalries in athletics.

The first notable meeting between Coe and Ovett came in the 800m final of the Moscow Olympics in 1980. Coe, the record-holder, was naturally favourite, but he was unaccountably out of sorts on the day of the race. 'I've never known pressure like it,' he said at the time, and afterwards admitted that he could barely remember the race. Ovett took his time entering the arena, but once on the starting blocks ran the race of his life, beating Coe easily. Coe was devastated. On the rostrum, Ovett offered his hand, which Coe took 'as if he'd just been handed a turd', as Clive James (then television critic for *The Observer*) famously commented. But Coe

had his revenge in the 1,500m six days later.

Both athletes had their ardent supporters, and a meeting between them was of intense national interest – more than 20 million people watched the race in Moscow, the broadcast interrupting the BBC's *Nine O'Clock News*. Advised by his coach (his father, Peter) to stick to Ovett come what may, Coe came off the final bend with Ovett at his shoulder and kicked for the tape, taking the East German, Jurgen Straub, in the final few metres and claiming the gold medal.

Although they met only seven times (one of those a schools cross-country race), each encounter was a milestone in athletics history. In 1981 the two men trumped each other's world records for the 1,500m three times.

Seb Coe raises a hand to salute the crowd as he wins the 1,500m in 1984, and with it his second Olympic gold medal.

In 1983, Coe contracted toxoplasmosis, a relatively rare blood disease, and his appearance in the 1984 Games looked in doubt after he had lost almost a year of training. But he recovered in time for the trials. Losing to Peter Elliott in the 1,500m trials, he was nonetheless (and somewhat controversially) selected.

At Los Angeles, Ovett had collapsed in the heats, and Coe met another old rival in the form of Steve Cram, but succeeded in taking the 1,500m gold medal, as well as silver in the 800m. Illness again forced him to miss the 1986 Commonwealth Games, but at the European Championships he took the 800m title, and finished second to Cram in the 1,500m.

Throughout his athletics career Coe had taken an active interest in politics, to which he turned on his retirement in 1990. In 1992, he became Conservative MP for Falmouth and Camborne. He became William Hague's chief of staff in his period of office as Conservative leader, but New Labour's sweeping electoral victory in 1997 persuaded Coe that it was time to leave front-line politics.

Coe was Vice Chairman of the Sports Council from 1986 to 1989, led London's bid to stage the 2000 Games, and in 2003 became an ambassador for the 2012 Games effort and a member of the organising board. In 2005 he became the Chairman of the London Organising Committee. His presentation at the critical IOC meeting in 2005 was said to be instrumental in the success of the bid.

He was also elected a vice president of the International Association of Athletics Federations and on 25 August 2011, was re-elected for another four-year term.

As 'an outstanding personality in the world of sport, a great personality in the Olympic movement,' in the words of FIFA President Sepp Blatter, in September 2006 Coe was appointed the first chairman of FIFA's ethics commission. He stood down from this post to join the England 2018 committee in an (unsuccessful) attempt to bring the World Cup to England. (Perhaps football is not really his thing – in September 2008 he controversially told reporters 'Fuck 'em!' when asked about the reported opposition to the creation of a footballing Team GB from Scottish and Welsh supporters.)

In recognition of his talent and services to sport, Coe was awarded the MBE in 1982 and OBE in 1990, and was created a life peer in 2000 as Baron Coe of Ranmore in the County of Surrey. He was further recognised by a Special Award at the BBC Sports Personality of the Year ceremony in 2005, and made a KBE in 2006.

In 2008, while Coe was at the Beijing Olympics, his father, who had been a huge influence on his career, died. 'The best middle distance coach in the world', Coe called him.

Coe was married to former eventer Nicky McIrvine, with whom he has four children. The couple divorced in 2002, and in 2011 he married Carole Annett, with whom has lived since 2003. He is a worldwide ambassador for Nike, owns a string of health clubs and is a member of the exclusive East India Club.

An outstanding athlete, successful politician and businessman, and a powerful force in the Olympic movement, Seb Coe is known throughout the world of sport and beyond. Rich, focused, determined, energetic and ambitious, he is in danger of becoming a national treasure.

Robin Cousins

1980 Lake Placid
Figure Skating

Robin Cousins has had a highly successful and diverse career, not only as a top British skater, but also as a choreographer, producer, director, costume designer, author, actor and artist. His superb free skating routine at Lake Placid, which included five triple jumps (more than any other competitor) earned him Olympic gold.

Cousins won his first title at the age of 12, made his international debut aged 14 and joined the British international team at 15. He won the National Senior Championships four years running and the World Free Skating Championships gold medal three times. He was British champion four times.

He has performed in numerous shows, tours and television ice specials as well as having his own successful touring ice shows, *Electric Ice* and *Ice Majesty*. His choreographic credits include *Starlight Express on Ice* and *The Wizard of Oz on Ice*, to name but two. All this as well as appearing in pantomime and presenting and commentating for BBC TV and NBC in America.

Knee and back problems forced Cousins to retire from skating in 2000, but he remains involved in the sport, continuing to produce, direct and choreograph, and appearing in musical theatre. That year he formed his own company, Cousins Entertainment Ltd, an event production company which also supplies and manages ice rinks.

Cousins was awarded the MBE in 1980. He is a judge of ITV's *Dancing on Ice*. He has been voted BBC Sports Personality of the Year and was inducted into the World Figure Skating Hall of Fame in 2005.

Robin Cousins smiles as he displays his gold medal won in the men's figure skating competition on 21 February 1980 in Lake Placid.

Duncan Goodhew
1980 Moscow
Swimming, 100m Breaststroke

Ranked by Channel 4 as one of the 100 Greatest Sporting Moments, Duncan Goodhew's victory in the final of the 100m breaststroke in Moscow made him a national hero. With his bald head and muscular body, Goodhew was instantly recognisable, and with an individual gold and a bronze medal from the 4x100m medley relay he became a household name. His hero status was cemented in 2000 when he saved the life of Labour MP Robert Sheldon with a textbook resuscitation from a heart attack.

Goodhew was also the first Briton to receive his medal to the strains of the national anthem and with the raising of the Olympic flag. He was also chosen as one of the torchbearers when the Olympic flame reached London on its journey to Beijing in 2008.

Goodhew's path to Olympic fame was not without its difficulties. His school days were made miserable by the fact that he was dyslexic and bald. A fall from a tree when he was eleven caused the rare and permanent condition alopecia universalis, and his dyslexia was not diagnosed until he was 13, by which time he had been dubbed 'Duncan the Dunce' by his peers. Swimming was a way out of the stress of academic life, and his complete lack of hair gave him a fractional advantage in the water. But it was not until he went to Millfield School in Somerset that his potential was recognised. He was spotted by Britain's swimming coach at the time, Paddy Garrett, who remarked prophetically, 'He'll swim for the school, he'll swim for the district, he'll swim for the county and he'll go beyond that'. While still at school, Goodhew was selected for the 1976 Olympics, finishing seventh in the 100m breaststroke.

Leaving Millfield on the premature death of his father, Goodhew won a scholarship to North Carolina State University and went to America to train and race. He went on to win three silver medals in the 1978 Commonwealth

The unmistakeable pate of Duncan Goodhew as he goes for gold in 1980.

Games and bronze in the World and European Championships. As the 1980 Olympics approached, his chance of Olympic gold looked in doubt after the boycott of the Games by many countries in protest at the Soviet invasion of Afghanistan. The American government imposed a total boycott, and UK Prime Minister Margaret Thatcher asked the British athletes to follow suit. The British Olympic Association opted to attend, and Goodhew had his chance.

Goodhew, like his hero Mark Spitz, retired at the peak of his career, but he went on to represent Great Britain in the 2- and 4-man bobsleigh teams at the European Championships.

He was awarded the MBE, became involved in the highly successful BT Swimathon which has raised over £10m for charity, and took up motivational speaking and writing – the delightfully-titled *The Self-help Book for Men Who Never Read Them,* and *Sink or Swim* drawing on his own life and the dedication and hard work required to succeed in any field. He continues to raise money for charity through swimming events and to inspire youngsters to take up the sport, which he calls the best strategy for all-round health and fitness. 'Whether you're in chlorine or salt water, you can see it, hear it, smell it and taste it – and every square inch of your skin feels it.'

Steve Ovett
1980 Moscow
Athletics, 800m

In the 1970s and '80s, a golden era of British middle-distance running, Steve Ovett's rivalry with Seb Coe was meat and drink to the media. Their contrasting characters – Ovett rough and streetwise, Coe suave and gentlemanly – and their determination to outdo each other was hyped by the press and caught the public interest, and each had a massive partisan following.

Ovett, the original 'bad boy' of athletics, showed precocious talent as a teenager. A promising footballer, he decided instead to concentrate on athletics since he preferred individual sport to those in which he was reliant on teammates. Between the ages of 15 and 19 he set records for his age every year at 800m, his favourite distance. At the age of 18 he won the European Junior

title with a record time, and came second in the event at senior level the following year in Rome. Already known for his burst of speed in the final straight, he got a place in the British team for the 1976 Games in Montreal, and came fifth. This turbojet kick in the last 200 metres of the inaugural IAAF World Cup gave him a famous win over the Olympic champion, John Walker, and really brought him to the public's attention.

The 1978 European Championships saw the first senior meeting between the two great rivals. An unexpected burst from the East German, Olaf Beyer, relegated Ovett to second place, with Coe third. But Ovett recovered to win the 1,500m, so far ahead of the field that he eased off before the tape to wave to the crowd. In the following seasons Ovett achieved record times in the 800m and 2-mile races.

With Ovett and Coe both in the squad for the 1980 Olympics, the media spotlight was on them for the showdown. Though not fancied to win the 800m, Ovett surprised everyone, particularly Coe, by taking him on the inside and beating him. When Ovett offered his hand at the medal presentation, Coe took it 'as if he'd just been handed a turd', as Clive James famously commented. Coe got his own back in the 1,500m, taking the gold medal, with Ovett only managing the bronze. (I know I've said that already, but it's too good not to repeat!)

During the season following the Olympics the two were at their peak, although they never met in a race. In the space of ten days they exchanged the world mile record three times.

For most of 1982 and early 1983, Ovett was out of competition through injury, but when fitness returned he broke the 1,500m world record with a time of 3:30.77.

In the run-up to the 1984 Games, in spite of intensive winter training in Australia, Ovett was still dogged by minor injuries and went into the competition with bronchitis. In trying to defend his 800m Olympic title he only narrowly qualified for the final, and when he finished in fourth place he collapsed and was taken to hospital. Unwisely, but with characteristic grit, he returned to compete in the 1,500m. In the last lap he dropped out, collapsed again and was stretchered off.

Although he won the 5,000m at the Commonwealth Games in 1986, Ovett's days at the top of his sport were over. He retired in 1991 and emigrated to Australia, where he is a sports adviser and television commentator. A statue of him, erected in Brighton in 1987, was stolen in 2007 and has yet to be replaced.

Steve Ovett storms ahead to win the 800 metres final at the Moscow Olympics, Sebastian Coe (254) in his wake. Nikolai Kirov (707) takes the bronze.

Daley Thompson
1980 Moscow and 1984 Los Angeles
Athletics, Decathlon

'Competition is my life,' said Daley Thompson, one of the world's greatest decathletes. 'Winning is my only goal. Everything I do is directed towards that end.' His dedication to sport has made him the most successful decathlete in history and earned him five gold medals in World, European and Olympic events as well as three Commonwealth Games titles.

When he refused to carry the Union Jack at the opening ceremony of 1984 Games for fear that

the effort would reduce his chances of winning a medal, he was criticised in some quarters. In sporting circles he was known to be brusque to the point of rudeness, but his talent, success and good looks ensured his popularity throughout his career. These attributes also hugely increased the appeal of the decathlon itself, as did his irreverent attitude – whistling the national anthem after getting his medal, swearing on television, and other such stunts.

Thompson competed in the first of his four Olympics as an 18-year-old in 1976 in Montreal. He returned in 1980 to take his first gold medal, and won again in 1984 to become only the second person in Olympic history to claim two decathlon gold medals.* By this time he had been unbeaten in decathlons for six years.

At the end of 1983, Thompson was at his peak. He was European, World, Commonwealth and Olympic champion, the first athlete to hold the titles simultaneously. Going into the Los Angeles Games he had lost his world title to his long-time rival, Jürgen Hingsen of West Germany, but from the start of the competition, Thompson was ahead. In the 1,500m final, he eased off at the finish and looked like missing out on regaining

*The first to do so was American Bob Mathias, 1948 & 1952.

Daley Thompson composes himself for the javelin during the 1984 decathlon.

the world record. When the photo-finish pictures were studied, however, it was found that he had been awarded a point too few in the 100m hurdles, and was thus equal record holder with Hingsen. When new scoring tables were subsequently introduced, Thompson's score totalled 8,847 points, a world record that stood until 1992.

Thompson has won every major title open to him and broken the world decathlon record four times. 'The most competitive sporting animal I have ever come across,' is how Frank Dick, the British athletics coach, described him.

He was awarded the MBE in 1982, the OBE in 1986, then the CBE in 2000. He was voted BBC Sports Personality of the Year in 1982. In 1992 a recurring hamstring injury forced Thompson to retire from athletics, but he played professional football for Mansfield Town and Stevenage Borough, and worked as fitness coach for Wimbledon and Luton Town.

He is an ambassador for the London 2012 Olympics Games – one of many appointed in 2008 to inspire people to become volunteers, coaches and mentors for young athletes around the UK. He's also been signed up test the Olympic torch in NMW's new Energy and Environmental Test Centre extreme weather facility – and who better to do it: the man is a legend.

Allan Wells
1980 Moscow
Athletics, 100m

Scotsman Allan Wells went into the Moscow Olympics at the relatively late age of 28 with high hopes. With two successful seasons behind him, and in spite of being obliged to use the novelty of starting blocks under the new Olympic regulations, he triumphed in the 100m sprint in a thrilling photo-finish race. Having qualified with a new British record time of 10.11 seconds, he was drawn on the outside with the favourite, Silvio Leonard of Cuba, on the inside. Twenty metres from the line, with the rest of the field beaten, Wells and Leonard were neck and neck – first Wells edging ahead, then Leonard. With seven metres to go Wells leaned hard. Both finished with a time of 10.25, but Wells' lean was just enough to get his head and shoulders past the tape ahead of Leonard's chest. In winning the gold medal, Wells became the oldest Olympic 100m champion, the first Briton to win it for 56 years, and – to date – the last white man to win the event.

In the 200m Wells came close to taking another gold medal. Though setting a British record of 20.21, he lost by 0.02 seconds to the Italian Pietro Mennea. He then participated in breaking a third British record with the sprint relay team, which finished fourth.

As a result of the Soviet invasion of Afghanistan in 1979, and various countries' moves to boycott the Moscow Games, it was felt by some that the medals were devalued. The fact that Wells went on to beat all the top athletes of the world in subsequent years, as well as the number of records broken in Moscow – 73 Olympic, 36 world and 29 European – tends to disprove such a contention.

Wells started his athletics career as a jumper. He was Scottish junior triple jump champion in 1970, and Scottish indoor long jump champion in 1974. In 1976 he decided to concentrate on the sprint, and by the following year he had won the Amateur Athletic Association 60m indoor title and the Scottish outdoor title – the first of seven such wins. Success after success followed: two gold medals and a silver at the 1978 Commonwealth Games and gold and bronze at the 1979 European Cup.

With his two medals from Moscow, Wells was firmly established as one of the world's greatest sprinters. He returned for his second Olympics in 1984, but failed to win a medal, and injury prevented him competing through most of 1985. But although in his thirties, Wells was not done, and came back to beat the 100m and 200m Commonwealth champions at Gateshead, as well as coming a respectable fifth at the Commonwealth Games. By the time he retired, Wells had won ten gold medals, six silver and two bronze.

Allan Wells was a trendsetter. He was the first athlete to adopt the now ubiquitous lycra running shorts, which led to him being dubbed 'Wilson of the Wizard', after a 1940s comic book character who wore a tight-fitting costume. More significantly for the sport, he was the first to concentrate his training on upper-body strength. His strenuous workouts included bench presses, speedball and press-ups, and his success in sustaining speed and rhythm throughout a race and the strength that allowed his trademark dip and lean, was to lead others, particularly Linford Christie, to emulate his impressive upper-body development.

After retiring from sprinting Wells became coach for the British bobsleigh team, and now coaches the Bank of Scotland specialist sprint team. His medal-winning times in the 100m and 200m at Moscow remain Scottish records.

Allan Wells gives a clenched-fist salute after winning the 100m gold medal in 1980.

Steve Redgrave

1984 Los Angeles, 1988 Seoul, 1992 Barcelona, 1996 Atlanta and 2000 Sydney
Rowing, Coxed Fours (1984), Coxless Pairs (1988, 1992 & 1996), Coxless Fours (2000)

When describing Sir Steven Redgrave one quickly runs out of superlatives. The most titled rower in history, the man is a towering figure, in stature and in his standing in the world of sport. Nine times winner of the World Championship in pairs or fours, three times winner of the World Cup, three times Commonwealth Champion, and our only athlete ever to win gold medals at five consecutive Games, he is justly hailed as Britain's greatest-ever Olympian.

Voted the greatest moment in British sporting history in a Channel 4 poll, more than 6.5m viewers tuned in to watch the final of the coxless fours in Sydney. No one would regret staying up until the early hours as the British team scraped home in a nail-biting photo-finish win over the battling Italians. Having made history at the age of 38, the exhausted Redgrave was ecstatic. When the crew, Redgrave, Pinsent, Foster and Cracknell, received their gold medals from the Princess Royal, Redgrave was also given a gold Olympic pin by the IOC President, to mark his outstanding achievement. He later said, 'Sure, it was desperate and fraught at the end, but we never doubted we would win. It was close, but that doesn't matter. Second best is not good enough, it's who crosses the line first.'

Redgrave has won so many events that there is no room here to list them all, but they include a record 23 titles at Henley, an Olympic bronze medal in 1988 to add to the five Olympic golds, as well as two silvers and a bronze to add to his nine World Championships between 1986 and 1999.

Of course, he did not achieve all this unaided, but he certainly knew how to choose his coaches

Sir Steven Redgrave celebrates gold with his son Zac after victory in the coxless fours final at the Sydney Games.

and his teammates. One of the latter, Matthew Pinsent, has since equalled his tally of world and Olympic medals. The others who contributed to his Olympic success were Andy Holmes, Adrian Ellison, Richard Budgett, Martin Cross, Patrick Sweeney, Tim Foster and James Cracknell.

The story of Redgrave's accomplishments does not end there: in 1989 he was a member of the British bobsleigh team, as well as national champion; he has run three marathons; in 1996 he won the UK Celebrity Gladiators competition. He was awarded first the MBE (1993), then the CBE (1997) and in 2001 was knighted. All this from a man who is dyslexic, diabetic, has ulcerative colitis and who famously said in 1996 that if anyone found him close to a rowing boat again, they could shoot him.

Redgrave retired from rowing in 2000 and was voted BBC Sports Personality of the Year. He took part in a three-part BBC documentary entitled *Gold Fever*, which had followed the coxless fours in the build-up to the Sydney Games.

A keen and competitive golfer, in 2009 he broke his leg falling down a grass bank after a pro-am European Masters game. He then drove 90 minutes home to watch the Champions League final before finally setting off for hospital.

Although he still enjoys rowing, his life now is filled with public speaking, PR and charity work. The Sir Steve Redgrave Charitable Trust (now the Steve Redgrave Fund) was launched in 2001, and has teamed up with Sport Relief and Comic Relief to raise money for young sportsmen and women. *Great Olympic Moments* was published in 2011 (his sixth book, and who better to write such a work?)

As if that wasn't enough, he took up canoeing in 2011 and in 2012 entered the gruelling Devizes to London race. He and his friend Roger Hatfield managed 87 miles of the 127-mile course before exhaustion got the better of them.

Having carried the flag at two Olympic opening ceremonies, at the time of writing Redgrave is 2/1 favourite to light the Olympic flame at the end of the 2012 torch relay.

'I'm just an ordinary guy who went quite quick in a boat, really,' he said. But to us mere mortals there is nothing ordinary about Sir Steve, the consummate competitor and true sporting hero.

Redgrave sporting his impressive tally of five gold medals from five separate Olympic Games.

Tessa Sanderson
1984 Los Angeles
Athletics, Javelin

Tessa Sanderson, the first female British black Olympic medallist, competed in six consecutive Olympic Games starting in 1976. She remains the only female British athlete to win an Olympic throwing gold medal. In an outstanding career spanning 26 years, she won ten Women's Amateur Athletic Association titles, a World Cup and three Commonwealth gold medals.

Born in Jamaica of Ghanaian parents, Sanderson was brought up by her grandmother and came to England at the age of nine. Settling in the Midlands, she showed considerable ability in junior pentathlon events. It became apparent early on that her particular strength lay in throwing the javelin. She hit her peak in the 1970s, but her position as Britain's foremost javelin thrower was usurped in the 1980s by Fatima Whitbread, with whom she shared a close rivalry for many years. Having failed to make the final at the 1980 Moscow Games, she then lost 21 of her first 22 contests against Whitbread. With such poor form she was not expected to shine at the Los Angeles Games, but with her first throw she set a new Olympic record of 69.56m and eventually took the gold medal, beating Whitbread into third place. 'All I wanted to do was throw the thing like almighty hell. And that's exactly what I did.'

In 1991, after a disappointing performance in the European championships, Sanderson took a break from athletics, but returned for the 1992 Games in Barcelona,

Tessa Sanderson in Atlanta in 1996 – her sixth Olympic appearance.

where she finished fourth. In the same year she won a gold medal at the World Cup, and turned her back on athletics in favour of a media career. Over the years, she has been a regular on BBC, ITV, GMTV, Sky and many other television and radio stations – as a presenter, panellist, guest and even on Channel 4's *Wife Swap* reality show with football manager Ron Atkinson (which recorded the highest viewing figures of the show!).

Then, in 1996, at the age of 40, she returned for her sixth Olympic appearance in Atlanta, but was eliminated in the qualifying round.

The Tessa Sanderson Foundation and Academy was founded in 2008 to help London youngsters, able and disabled, to enjoy all sports and participate at a higher level without jeopardising their education.

For her sporting achievements and Vice Chairmanship of Sport England, as well as her tireless work for charities, Sanderson was awarded the CBE in 2004. She was appointed to the board of the Olympic Park Legacy Company (formed to oversee the formation of the Olympic Park for the Newham community and people in the East End of London), but in 2011 resigned over the proposed use of the Olympic Stadium as a football ground.

Much in demand as a motivational speaker, there's no doubt that Sanderson has passion, personality and pizzazz to spare.

Malcolm Cooper
1984 Los Angeles and 1988 Seoul
Shooting, 50m Rifle Three Positions

Malcolm Cooper is widely acknowledged as the finest marksman of his day. In all, he won a total of 149 medals – 61 at Olympic, European or World Championships – and broke or equalled 13 world records.

Cooper took up shooting when his father, a lieutenant in the Royal Navy, was posted to New Zealand. Following the family's return to England, Malcolm became a shipwright's apprentice in Portsmouth and joined the HMS Nelson Rifle Club. In 1970 he made it into the British team, going on to win the national three positions (prone, standing and kneeling) title 12 times.

Utterly single-minded and dedicated to his sport, Cooper trained hard, swimming 30 lengths a day and running miles. He and his wife, Sarah Robinson (at one time British women's shooting champion and a team member in Seoul), shunned all distractions in the pursuit of excellence. They had no children, pets or television. His finest year was possibly 1985, when he won all five events at the European Championships.

The British government's decision to boycott the 1980 Moscow Olympics in protest at the Soviet invasion of Afghanistan did not prevent individual sports bodies entering if they wished. The National Small-bore Rifle Association upheld the boycott and Cooper was thus denied an almost certain gold medal. But in 1984 he achieved his aim when he scored a record 1,173 points out of 1,200, shooting for five hours in searing temperatures. He returned to the Olympics in 1988 in Seoul and became the only person successfully to defend the title, in spite of having his rifle damaged by a BBC cameraman just before the competition. Ironically, the weapon was repaired by a Russian armourer.

He retired from the sport in 1991, concentrating on developing Accuracy International, an engineering company manufacturing precision rifles which he had established in 1978. The company had helped fund his Olympic ambitions, and in 1998 won the Queen's Award for Export. By 1990, he was supplying the British army with their standard sniper rifles.

Cooper was awarded the MBE in 1984. He was President of the Havant Rifle and Pistol Club from 1988 until his death from cancer in 2001. In recognition of his status as Britain's greatest shooter, a range at the National Shooting Centre in Bisley is named after him.

Malcolm Cooper, double gold medallist and the world's finest marksman in his day.

Christopher Dean and Jayne Torvill
1984 Sarajevo
Figure Skating, Ice Dancing

The partnership of Torvill and Dean is one of the world's best-known sporting pairings and their faultless routine in the 1984 Olympic ice dance final will go down in history as the most brilliant skating performance ever, and one of the most popular in British sport. Watched by a television audience of over 24 million, the pair received a record perfect score for artistic impression from all nine judges, who gave them the highest overall score of all time for their interpretation of Ravel's *Bolero*.

The two skaters teamed up in 1975, when Dean was in the police force and Torvill was already a British junior champion, winning their first trophy in their second year together. They attended the Olympics and World Championships in 1980, finishing fifth and fourth respectively, and thereafter won medals in every World and British Championships until 1996, usually coming first. Coached by Betty Callaway from 1978, and mentored by the singer-actor Michael Crawford from 1981, the two turned professional in 1984. In 1994, thanks to a relaxation of the rules, they were able to revert temporarily to amateur status to enter the 1994 Games in Lillehammer, where they took the bronze medal.

Much as the media would have liked it, the two had no romantic entanglement. In 1998 Torvill and Dean retired from competition, though they continued to perform together in ice dance extravaganzas, notably ITV's *Dancing on Ice*, for some years afterwards, by which time both were married.

In 1982 and 1983 the pair won the Sports Team of the Year award, and in 1984 were named Sports Personalities of the Year. In 1981 they were each awarded the MBE and then OBE in 2000. Between them, Torvill and Dean took ice dancing to a new level, proving an almost unbeatable combination and becoming the darlings of the media. Their remarkable achievements have been acknowledged in their home town of Nottingham, where a number of roads are named after them. They were inducted into the World Figure Skating Hall of Fame in 1989.

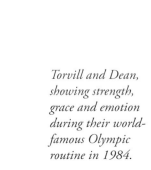

Torvill and Dean, showing strength, grace and emotion during their world-famous Olympic routine in 1984.

Sean Kerly
1988 Seoul
Field Hockey

Sean Kerly is one of Britain's best-known sportsmen and surely its best-known hockey player, described by the press as 'the Gary Lineker of hockey'. As top scorer at Seoul he rocketed to fame in a sport that had hitherto received little attention but in 1988 captivated millions of British television viewers. When the team beat the West Germans 3-1, with a goal from Kerly and two from Imran Sherwani, to take Britain's third hockey gold medal, the nation rejoiced. And where *were* the Germans?

Kerly, Sherwani and Steve Batchelor formed the backbone of the British team at their three Olympic appearances. For their efforts in 1984 and 1988 the team were awarded the BBC Sports Personality of the Year award, and Kerly was nominated for an individual award in 1988. Having quit his job as a marketing manager to train for the 1988 Games, he found it hard to adjust to the media attention and champagne receptions, the visits to Buckingham Palace and 10 Downing Street, the awards and accolades. He did some public speaking, some television appearances, even had a walk-on part in a pantomime, and eventually settled down and returned to full-time work. He now runs a graphic art and marketing agency.

In an outstanding career, Kerly made 74 appearances for Great Britain, scored 57 goals, and played in 58 outdoor and nine indoor internationals for England. He scored seven goals for the bronze medal-winning team in Los Angeles, and eight at the Seoul Games. He

Sean Kerly leaps in the air as Great Britain beat the Germans in the 1988 hockey final. The clinching third goal prompted the famous comment by commentator Barry Davies: 'And where were the Germans? And quite frankly, who cares?'

won silver medals at the 1986 World Cup and the 1987 European Cup, and was a member of the Southgate team which won the English Club Championships in 1987 and 1988.

Kerly puts his success down to 'hard work, enthusiasm, bloody-mindedness and a very good team around me'. He retired in 1992 and was awarded the MBE. He appeared frequently on *Grandstand*, and was part of the BBC's commentary team for the Atlanta and Beijing Olympics.

Linford Christie
1992 Barcelona
Athletics, 100m

There can be few more controversial British Olympians than Linford Christie, a man of immense talent and deep grievances. A world-class sprinter and winner of more medals than any other British male athlete, Christie is the only man in history to hold the Olympic, World, European and Commonwealth titles for the 100m, but mention his name and the immediate associations are 'lunchbox', 'drugs cheat', and running feuds with the establishment.

Born in Jamaica, Christie followed his parents to London when he was seven. At school he was a good all-rounder, but did not take up athletics seriously until he was 19, by which time he had sown a good number of wild oats and fathered three children. Failure to make the sprint relay team for the 1984 Games goaded him to train in earnest and in 1986 he won the European Championship 100m and came second at the Commonwealth Games.

At the Olympics in 1988 he earned his first Olympic medal, a silver, and his first positive drugs test. By a margin of eleven to ten, the IOC voted to clear him (although two of the judges were said to be asleep during the vote). In 1991 at the World Championships in Tokyo he took part in one of the greatest 100m races in memory when, for the first and only time, six men broke

the mystical ten-second barrier in the same race. It was won by Carl Lewis, and Christie, in spite of breaking his European record by 0.05 seconds, came only fourth.

In 1992, Christie achieved his ambition of Olympic gold, winning the 100m final in a time of 9.96 seconds. At the comparatively late age of 32 he became the oldest Olympic 100m champion. After a bumper year in 1993, taking the four major titles and becoming BBC Sports Personality of the Year, he returned to the Games

Linford Christie celebrates after running the anchor leg to take the silver medal in the 4x100m relay in Seoul.

in 1996, but was disqualified in the final after two false starts.

It was Christie's late flowering that led to the court case against John McVicar, the journalist and ex-con. McVicar had accused Christie in print of being a drugs cheat, questioning how he could have risen from 156th to fourth in one year of sprinting without taking drugs.

Christie sued for libel and won. During the trial Christie let loose a tirade about the media's treatment of him, particularly their comments about his manhood and the running joke about his 'lunchbox'. To everyone's amusement, Mr Justice Popplewell had to have the term explained.

Having won his libel action, Christie was to be convicted of doping in 1999 in Germany when he was semi-retired and in the twilight of his career. Found guilty of taking the performance-enhancing drug nandrolone, Christie strenuously denied and continues to deny the charge. Although the verdict of the UK Athletics body was that there was reasonable doubt, the International Association of Athletics Federations handed Christie a two-year ban, and the British

Olympic Association announced he would not be accredited for any future Olympics. At the time, Christie was publicly slated by Sebastian Coe, which led to a long and bitter feud. In 2008, he was snubbed by the London Olympic Organising Committee – first invited by Mayor Ken Livingstone to be a torchbearer, only to have the offer withdrawn – and the feud reached new heights. Christie blamed Coe for the rejection, launching a furious attack: 'I have nothing good to say about Sebastian Coe at all, absolutely nothing'. He went on to blame institutional racism within the BOA for the fact that he had not received a knighthood.

In spite of all, Christie must remain one of the most talented and successful British athletes. And while he 'swears on his children's lives' that he never took drugs, he has found a measure of peace. He cooks, he gardens (and once did a series for the BBC), cares for his five children and has made a name for himself coaching the likes of Darren Campbell and Katharine Merry. And if he didn't receive the knighthood he thought he deserved, at least he has a stadium in west London named after him.

Chris Boardman (see next page) on his revolutionary Lotus Superbike as he heads for victory in the individual pursuit final in 1992.

Chris Boardman
1992 Barcelona
Cycling, Individual Pursuit

In spite of winning only one Olympic gold medal, Chris Boardman is one of the most famous of all cyclists. At the Barcelona Olympics, Boardman's revolutionary cycle, designed by Mike Burrows and built by Lotus, caused a sensation. The new 'superbike' overturned bicycle design – the frame and forks were dramatically different, and it had a lenticular wheel at the back made largely of carbon fibre. It also sported a tri-bar, a handlebar used in the triathlon and designed to reduce the cyclist's wind profile. The bike weighed less than 20lbs and took Boardman to two world records in the preliminary rounds. In the final, he did what no man has ever done before or since in an Olympic 4,000m pursuit final – he lapped his rival. It was Britain's first cycling gold medal since 1920.

A specialist in the individual time trial, Boardman won his first title in the 1984 GHS schoolboy 10-mile championship (an event named for George Herbert Stancer, the renowned cyclist of the mid-1900s). That year he also broke the junior 25-mile national record, going on to win the 1986 junior 25-mile championship. As a senior, he won the hill climb championships four years in succession (1988–1991), five consecutive 25-mile championships (1989–1993), the 50-mile championship in 1991 and 1992, and the men's British time trial championship in 2000. He broke the 25-mile record again in 1992 and 1993 and, as a member of the North Wirral Velo team, broke the 100km team time trial record in 1993 with a time of 2:00.07. In all, he won over 30 national titles. He turned professional in 1993 and joined the French team Gan, winning the Grand Prix Eddy Merckx in Brussels.

He came to public notice again in 1994 when he won the prologue of the Tour de France in the fastest time ever recorded, but he may be better remembered for breaking the world one-hour record, a blue riband event in cycling, three times.

Altogether Boardman has been engaged in six Olympic Games, as a competitor from 1988 to 2000 (one gold, and a bronze medal in Atlanta in the road race) and most recently in Beijing as part of the 2008 cycling management team.

In 1998, Boardman was diagnosed with a form of osteoporosis. The treatment involved the use of testosterone, a banned substance in sport. Boardman chose to postpone treatment and to continue cycling. In 2000 he decided to retire, ending his phenomenal career with an attempt at a new one-hour record. He reportedly shaved his entire body to increase his chances. In front of a huge crowd, he set a record of 30.723 miles in an hour, beating Eddy Merckx's 1972 distance of 30.716 miles.

Since 2002 Boardman has been Director of Research and Development for British Cycling, and the   haul of 14 British Olympic cycling medals in 2008 owes much to his management and technical skills. British Cycling will miss him when he stands down after the London Games.

Jonny and Greg Searle
1992 Barcelona
Rowing, Men's Coxed Pairs

When the crews lined up for the final of the coxed pairs in 1992, there was guarded hope that Great Britain might bag a medal but no great optimism that it would be gold. After all, the Searle brothers had only 8 races under their belts while the Italian Abbagnale brothers, seven times World Champions and double Olympic gold medallists, had more than 200 and had proved virtually unbeatable for years. The 2,000m race that followed took everyone's breath away. By the 1,000m mark, the Italians had opened up a length's lead; 250m from home there was still clear water between them and the Searles. With a superhuman effort, in a mere 25 strokes the battling Brits made up a whole length – and in the last seconds pulled ahead to take the gold medal.

The BBC commentator, Steve Ryder, not knowing he was still on air but echoing the thoughts of a nation, breathed, 'that was *unbelievable!*' 'Power, strength and, above all, courage', 'youth, vigour and steely determination', extolled the pundits.

Underlining their effort, cox Garry Herbert said: 'I wanted them to be prepared to die for us, and they nearly did'. His tear-stained face on the podium, splashed across the front and back pages of the press, said it all.

Back to the beginning: the Searle brothers attended Hampton School in Middlesex. Jonny took up rowing and Greg took up rugby, but when he saw his brother winning medals Greg switched to the water.

Jonny went up to Oxford and competed in the University Boat Race in 1988, 1989, and 1990 (winning each time). He became a litigation lawyer, juggling work, training and competition, with great success. He is Head of Legal and Business Affairs at Viasat Broadcasting and is involved with the Olympic and Paralympic Employment Network (OPEN).

While still at school, in 1988 Greg was selected for the coxed pair for the Junior World Championships, finishing fourth. In the next two years, as a member of the junior coxless four he became only the second British junior (after Tim Foster) to win two World Championships gold medals. He won his second junior gold in 1990 and became the first athlete to achieve selection for both senior and junior World Championships in the same year by gaining a seat in the men's eight alongside Jonny. The brothers raced together for the first time in the eights in 1990, coming fourth in the World Championships. In 1991 they took bronze, before switching to the coxed pairs in 1992.

Steve Gunn, who had coached the pair at Hampton School and at Molesey Boat Club, dropped everything to resume work with them after their victory over Steve Redgrave and Matthew Pinsent in the Olympic trials at Nottingham that April (Jonny had broken a rib in this race and only just got back to fitness in time for the Olympics). The gold medal was a great reward for his faith in them.

At the 1993 World Championships the Searles cemented their reputation by taking the coxed pairs title from the Abbagnales. The same year the brothers were awarded the MBE. The coxed pair had by then been removed from the Olympic programme and in 1994 both switched to the coxless four. They were joined by Tim Foster and fellow old-Hamptonian Rupert Obholzer with whom they had rowed in the 1991 eight. A bronze medal in the World Championships and a silver medal in 1995 (losing to the Italians), saw them in good form for the Atlanta Olympics in 1996. There, the Searles took the bronze medal.

In 1997 Greg converted briefly to the single scull and in 2000 he teamed up with Ed Coode in the coxless pairs. They made it to the Olympic final in Sydney, but in spite of leading most of the way, were beaten into fourth place.

A past President of Oxford Rowing Club and a Steward for Henley Royal Regatta, Jonny retired from rowing in 2000. Greg 'retired' in 2001 but...

On 2 August 2012, 20 years to the day since that memorable race, Greg Searle will return to the Olympics in the men's eight to strive for another gold medal. His performance in the World Cup in Belgrade in May 2012 (taking place as I write) shows that he is as fit and determined as ever. His talent and experience ('Grandad' to his fellow crew members) will be invaluable.

Cox Garry Herbert breaks down as he and Greg (left) and Jonny Searle take gold in the coxed pairs at the 1992 Barcelona Games.

Sally Gunnell
1992 Barcelona
Athletics, 400m Hurdles

Sally Gunnell, the archetypal 'girl next door', is a hugely popular and successful British sportswoman. The first British woman to win a hurdles gold medal at the Olympics, she is also the only woman to hold Olympic, World, European and Commonwealth titles concurrently. In all, she has won 13 gold medals in major championships. In Barcelona, as the team captain, she ran the race of her life to take the 400m hurdles gold medal in a nail-biting finish with the American Sandra Farmer-Patrick. She also won bronze in the 4x400m relay.

Gunnell began her athletics career in the long jump and pentathlon, but with her strength and stamina soon turned to hurdling. In 1986 she won the 100m hurdles at the Commonwealth Games,

Sally Gunnell proudly wears the flag after winning the 400m hurdles in Barcelona.

two years later setting a British record of 12.82. She moved up to the 400m hurdles and earned a place in the squad for the Seoul Olympics in 1988, where she finished fifth. By the Barcelona Games, Gunnell was in peak condition and her personal best was down to a time of 53.16. The electrifying final saw her triumph with a time of 53.23. In a rematch with Farmer-Patrick at the World Championships the following year, she won again in a time of 52.74 – the eighth time she had broken the British record. In 1994 she added the European and Commonwealth to her list of titles, before injury struck in 1995. Though she missed most of the season, she still made it on to the team for the Atlanta Games in 1996, but was forced to withdraw in the semi-finals. It was her 30th birthday; her Achilles tendon failed to see her through.

Gunnell retired in 1997, having served a year as a Red Cross ambassador in Angola. She was awarded the OBE in 1998 and went on to join the BBC as a trackside interviewer and pundit. After a certain amount of adverse comment in the press for her interviewing technique, she complained that the BBC had failed to support her and quit the £60,000 a year job in 2006.

Married to fellow-athlete Jonathan Bigg, she has three children and pursues a successful career as a motivational speaker. As well as being a keen horsewoman, she spearheads many charities and works with the British Heart Foundation and Sport England in improving the nation's fitness.

Matthew Pinsent
1992 Barcelona, 1996 Atlanta, 2000 Sydney and 2004 Athens
Rowing, Coxless Pairs (1992 & 1996), Coxless Fours (2000 & 2004)

Between 1991 and 2002 there was not a year in which Matthew Pinsent did not win a gold medal. But it was perhaps the final of the coxless fours in Athens that marked his most memorable victory, and was voted Britain's Greatest Sporting Moment that year. With the crowd on the edge of their seats, Pinsent, Coode, Cracknell and Williams battled the Canadians, swapping the

Pinsent wipes away a tear as the National Anthem is played for the winning coxless four of 2004: Matthew Pinsent (left), James Cracknell, Ed Coode and Steve Williams (right).

lead with almost every stroke as they powered to the finish. In a nail-biting photo-finish, the British crew won by 8/100th of a second with a last minute spurt. There were tears in Pinsent's eyes as he stood on the podium, and in those of most of the millions of British spectators. The magnanimous Canadian stroke, Barney Williams, said that if he had to lose, it was a privilege to lose to the world's greatest rower. Nor was there a dry eye in the British press contingent, one pundit going so far as to say, 'We who are about to cry, salute you!'

One of only five athletes to win four consecutive Olympic gold medals, Pinsent's partnerships first with Steve Redgrave and then James Cracknell have netted him an astonishing ten World Championship gold medals, an all-time record. Pinsent began rowing at Eton, coming fourth at the Junior World Championships in 1987 at the age of 16, and winning the junior coxless pair with Tim Foster in 1988. On going up to Oxford to study Geography, he teamed up with Steve Redgrave and they won the coxless pairs at the 1990 World Championships. It was the beginning of a phenomenally successful partnership, which saw them win the World Championships five times and Olympic gold three times, twice in the coxless pairs and once in the fours.

When Redgrave retired in 2000, Pinsent teamed up with James Cracknell and the medals kept coming. Undefeated in 2001, they completed the unique feat of winning the coxed pairs and, two hours later, the coxless pairs. Another year on and they successfully defended their title, breaking the world record by four seconds. In 2003 Pinsent's winning run was broken, and he and Cracknell switched to the men's coxless four, whereupon he stroked the crew to his fourth gold medal, Cracknell's second, and the first for Coode and Williams.

Another curious claim to fame is that, until he was recently outdone by fellow rower Peter Reed, Pinsent had the largest lung capacity ever recorded in Britain – 8.5 litres of air with every breath.

At the end of 2004 Pinsent retired from rowing, and was awarded a knighthood. In retirement he turned to broadcasting, as a sports bulletin presenter for BBC News, as well as working on the BBC series *Inside Sport*, and writing for *The Times* and *Racing News*. His autobiography, *A Lifetime in a Race*, was published in 2004.

In 2010 Sir Matthew was chosen as a torchbearer for the Vancouver Winter Olympics. The Canadians may have been a bit hazy about who he was as he ran his leg, but there is no doubt about the esteem and affection in which he is held by the Brits!

Ben Ainslie
2000 Sydney, 2004 Athens and 2008 Beijing
Sailing, Laser Class (2000), Finn Class (2004 & 2008)

Having sailed from the age of four, Ben Ainslie has become the most successful Finn Class sailor ever and, together with Rodney Pattisson, one of the most successful sailors in Olympic history, winning gold in three consecutive Games. Encouraged by his father Roddy, who had sailed in the first Whitbread Round the World Race of 1973–4, the young Ben began competing at the age of eight, and won a gold medal at the World Youth Championships in 1995 when he was 18 years old.

Having suffered most of his life with a skin photosensitivity which causes blisters and rashes on his face, Ainslie was picked on at school. The bullying, he says, made him 'ferociously determined to be good at something'. And at sailing he became ferociously good. He made his

Olympic debut in 1996 in Atlanta, the youngest British sailor to be selected for the Games, winning the silver in the Laser Class. In 1998 and 1999 he won the World Championships in this Class, and took his first gold at the 2000 Sydney Games, where his unorthodox blocking tactics (a retaliation against the Brazilian Robert Scheidt's dirty tricks in 1996) in the final race resulted in death threats. In 2002, having deliberately gained 18 kilos of weight, he moved to the larger Finn Class and won five World Championships, and gold medals in the 2004 and (in spite of contracting mumps days before) the 2008 Games. In 2009 he skippered the British team to victory in the King Edward VII Gold Cup, and in 2010, with TEAMORIGIN, won the World Championship and the Monsoon Cup.

Ben Ainslie holds the Union Flag aloft after winning his third gold medal in Beijing.

International sport today is a far cry from the state of play in the 19th, and even the 20th, century. The competition is fiercer, the training more gruelling and the financial rewards are enormous. With all the increased pressure and expectations, tempers frequently boil over, even in the most gentlemanly of sports. In December 2011, Ben Ainslie hit the headlines in a way he would have preferred to avoid. During the World Championships in Perth he was disqualified for diving into the water and accosting a television crew who, he claimed, had repeatedly interfered with the race. It was the final buffet from the camera craft as Ainslie crossed the line in second place that drove him over the edge, into the ocean and up into the TV boat, where gave them a mouthful, knocked one of them over and swam back to his own boat.

He was quick to apologise, saying it had taught him a lot about himself as well as making him stronger and more determined to be successful.

His return was hampered by a back injury, but in April 2012 he was back on form, winning the first European World Cup regatta of the season in Majorca, with a day to spare. A few weeks later he won his record sixth Finn World Championship title in Falmouth Bay, Cornwall.

In total, Ainslie has won ten World and nine European Championships and is the only sailor ever to be crowned ISAF World Sailor of the Year three times and British Yachtsman of the Year five times. He was inducted into the Finn Hall of Fame in 2004 and in 2008 a CBE was added to his earlier MBE and OBE.

He was chosen as skipper for the 33rd America's Cup British challenge in 2010. In January 2012 he launched Ben Ainslie Racing, a new team that will initially compete in the next edition of the America's Cup World Series.

A gold medal in 2012 – a highly likely occurrence – would make him the most successful sailor in Olympic history.

Stephanie Cook
2000 Sydney
Athletics, Modern Pentathlon

Described by the press as 'the thinking man's sporting pin-up', Steph Cook surprised the world by retiring from sport at the age of 29 at the height of her career to pursue her medical profession.

A committed Christian, she attended both Cambridge and Oxford, where she read medicine. Having rowed at Cambridge, and being already a competent rider, runner and swimmer, on going up to Oxford Cook quickly mastered the other disciplines in the pentathlon. She qualified as a doctor in 1997, and the following year won a team silver medal at the World Championships and an individual bronze.

The demands of training for five events with the Olympics in sight obliged Cook to put her medical career on hold. The decision paid dividends in the form of a gold medal in Sydney. In the final event, the 3km run, Cook made up a 49-second deficit and took the lead with only 250m to go, to clinch the victory. 'I remember running up towards the line and thinking my life is never going to be the same again,' she later said.

Cook's good looks and engaging personality, not to mention the gold medal, brought her instant fame and offers of radio and television appearances. She was unaffected by her celebrity status and the following year, 2001, she won individual gold medals at both the European and World Championships and was awarded the MBE for services to the modern pentathlon.

Cook cites Eric Liddell as a hero and inspiration, and, following his example, she retired in 2001. After relief work in Gujarat, India, helping the earthquake victims, she returned to her medical career.

[It is a mark of her personality that Dr Cook is the only athlete included in this book to acknowledge receipt of a copy of the first edition, with her thanks and amendments.]

A champagne moment for Steph Cook after winning the Modern Pentathlon World Championship in 2001.

Three Blondes in a Boat and the Yngling Girls

2000 Sydney, 2004 Athens and 2008 Beijing

Shirley Robertson (2000 Europe Class & 2004 Yngling Class);
Sarah Ayton (2004 & 2008 Yngling Class); Sarah Webb (2004 & 2008 Yngling Class);
Pippa Wilson (2008 Yngling Class)

The Yngling is a three-person boat with keel and three sails which replaced the Soling Class in Olympic sailing after the 2000 Sydney Games and was competed for in 2004 and 2008. Shirley Robertson was the senior member of the winning Yngling crew of 2004, both in age and experience. She had started sailing at the age of six in her native Scotland and at the age of 32 succeeded in winning her first gold medal at the 2000 Sydney Games in the single-handed Europe Class. She then teamed up with Sarah Ayton and Sarah Webb and the threesome won the first Olympic gold medal for the Yngling Class in Athens with a race to spare.

Known as the 'three blondes in a boat', the good-looking trio became overnight stars,

featured on the front and back pages of the newspapers, but their beaming faces masked the strains in their relationship. Robertson's strong leadership style from the helm was causing tension and dissension. The two Sarahs felt that they were merely the crew serving the master rather than a team of equals – Sarah Ayton, equally strong-minded, felt the subordination particularly keenly since she had been at the top of her profession since the age of 18. In spite of their triumph in Athens they decided to part company from Robertson.

It took some searching for Ayton and Webb to find a compatible third. Eventually Pippa Wilson, a successful 470 Class yachtswoman, was chosen and the team instantly bonded, with

The 'three blondes in a boat' share a joke after winning the Yngling Class race in Athens in 2004.

From left to right: Sarah Webb, Shirley Robertson and Sarah Ayton.

teamwork as their watchword. Ayton took over the helm and the trio ('three blondes in a boat: the sequel') knuckled down to training with the aim of beating Shirley Robertson and her new crew to the Yngling selection for the Beijing Games in 2008.

Robertson, meanwhile, was seeking new challenges in different types of craft, had embarked on a successful media career, and started a family. When her focus returned to the Olympics and the Yngling gold medal, she teamed up with Annie Lush and Lucy Macgregor. With only one boat per nation allowed to enter for the Olympics, the competition was intense and heightened by the rivalry and resentments between Robertson and Ayton. The showdown came at the World Championships in 2007 in Portugal. Ayton's crew dominated the event. In the final they still led, but with Robertson a close second. Approaching the mark at the top of the course Wilson fell overboard. She was quickly hauled back into the boat by Sarah Webb but valuable seconds had been lost. With Robertson breathing down their necks, Ayton, unperturbed, steered round the mark and they sailed on to

victory and selection for the Games. An unhappy Robertson complained she had been given too little time to prepare, and promptly sold her boat to the Americans. She attended the Beijing Games – as the BBC's sailing commentator and not, as she had hoped, on the water.

The conditions at the sailing venue 500 miles south of Beijing were to begin with so calm as to make sailing unexciting, and sometimes impossible. But on the day of the final, strong winds blew and the sea churned. Electing not to fight a tactical battle in such rough conditions, the 'Yngling girls' (as they were by now known) went out on their own and raced home to take the gold medal just seven seconds ahead of the Germans. It was the first gold for Pippa Wilson and the second for the Sarahs. On the dockside they were joined by Shirley Robertson, their differences temporarily forgotten in patriotic joy. Ayton's fiancé, Nick Dempsey, meanwhile was competing in the windsurfing event. With the Yngling Class dropped from the 2012 Olympics, Sarah Ayton teamed up with Saskia Clark in the double-handed 470 Class instead, with every intention of another gold medal attempt. But her marriage to Dempsey and the demands of motherhood led to her retirement from sailing in 2011. A great loss to the Olympic team.

The blonde yachtswomen were all rewarded with honours, Robertson, Ayton and Webb with the MBE and OBE, and Wilson with the MBE.

Pippa Wilson, Sarah Webb and Sarah Ayton on their way to overall victory in the Yngling Class event on day 9 of the Beijing Games in 2008.

James Cracknell
2000 Sydney and 2004 Athens
Rowing, Coxless Fours

Double Olympic Champion and World Record holder along with Matthew Pinsent, Cracknell is an inspirational sporting icon. His 13-year

James Cracknell, with determined expression, gives it his all during the British national team trials in 2004.

international career netted him two Olympic gold medals and six World Championships and has made him one of Britain's most successful athletes of all time.

He began his rowing career while at Kingston Grammar School and won his first gold medal in the Junior World Championships in 1990 as stroke of the British four. A hatful of medals followed: a total of six in the World Championships in coxless and coxed pairs and coxless fours. In 2001 Cracknell and Pinsent won the coxed and coxless pairs on the same day, and in 2002 smashed the world record in the coxless pairs by four seconds.

Cracknell's Olympic record is equally impressive. Although he qualified in the double scull for the 1996 Games, last minute tonsillitis prevented him racing. In 1997 he teamed up with Redgrave, Pinsent and Foster. The final of the coxless fours in Sydney was an event watched by millions around the world, a thrilling race which saw Redgrave win an historic fifth successive gold medal as the British held off the Italian challenge to win by 0.38 seconds. That race, with the lead up to it, was made into a three-part BBC documentary entitled *Gold Fever*.

Thrilling as the Sydney race was, the final in 2004 at Athens was one of the most exciting rowing contests ever seen. In a nail-biting contest with the Canadians, and the lead changing repeatedly in the final 500m, the British team edged home to win by a mere seven inches. After the race Cracknell said, 'When you put four years of emotion into six minutes, you end up in a scrambled heap'.

After retiring from rowing in 2006, Cracknell turned to journalism, and has carved out a distinguished career as a writer, presenter, speaker and all-round adventurer. As a presenter for ITV and Channel 4 he has covered such diverse sports as superbike, rugby sevens, the Red Bull Air Race World Series and of course the Boat Race. He also spent ten years as a sports feature writer for *The Daily Telegraph*.

The indefatigable Cracknell has done much to raise money for charity. In 2006 he and Ben Fogle entered the gruelling 3,000-mile Atlantic Rowing race in aid of BBC Children in Need. Having rowed naked much of the way, and capsized once, the pair came third. Their achievement is recorded in the BBC documentary *Through Hell and High Water*.

In 2008, to raise funds for Sport Relief, he set out to reach Africa in ten days by human power alone. He rowed the Channel, cycled more than 1,395 miles and swam the Strait of Gibraltar. In January 2009 he teamed up again with Ben Fogle and Ed Coats to take part in the Amundsen Omega 3 South Pole Race, coming an impressive second, only 20 hours behind the Norwegian long-distance ski experts. The event has been made into a six-part BBC TV series, *On Thin Ice*.

Having followed a punishing training schedule throughout his competitive career, Cracknell has been equally tireless since quitting rowing. As well as his journalistic and charitable works, and being a keen advocate of health and fitness, he is director of Threshold Sports, a consultancy service aimed at sustaining participation in sport.

Cracknell is married to TV and radio presenter Beverley Turner. He was honoured with the MBE in 2001 and the OBE in 2004, and appointed Sustainability Ambassador by the London Organising Committee of the 2012 Olympic Games.

There seems to be no limit to the man's energy and enthusiasm. In 2011 he entered the Marathon de Sable – the punishing 6-day, 151-mile endurance race across the Sahara Desert in Morocco. He finished 12th, becoming the highest-placed Briton in its 25-year history.

Barely pausing to rest, he then embarked on a new challenge, 'James Cracknell Takes on America', in which he was to cycle, run, row and swim from Los Angeles to New York. He was doing well and in Arizona when a petrol tanker hit him from behind, knocking him from his cycle, smashing his brain against the frontal lobes, and fracturing his skull in two places. 'I was lit up like a Christmas tree for God's sake. How didn't he see me?' he said, although grateful to the driver for at least stopping!

It was feared he would not survive. But, with characteristic resilience and determination, survive he did, and six months later (and after some extremely erratic behaviour) was found among the entrants in Yukon Arctic Ultra. Discovery Channel filmed his epic 430-mile journey – the *Coldest Race on Earth* – which Cracknell opted to tackle on a bicycle.

These last few exploits have been broadcast by Discovery Channel under the title *Unstoppable*.

Indeed, 'unstoppable' just about sums him up. From the Arctic to the South Pole, from Sahara to the States, in any temperature and across any terrain, Cracknell will tackle the challenge.

Jonathan Edwards
2000 Sydney
Athletics, Triple Jump

Jonathan Edwards, evangelical Christian turned atheist, is the undoubted king of the triple jump, widely regarded as the event's greatest champion. There are few titles he has not won, and his world record of 18.29m at the World Championships in 1995 has yet to be bettered – a huge jump which came immediately after a record-breaking first jump of over 18m. During that year he also set three world and seven British records, and his wind-assisted jump of 18.43m at the European Cup in Lille is the longest triple jump in history.

Jonathan Edwards looks to the heavens after winning the triple jump in Sydney in 2000. The world record distance he jumped in 1995 has yet to be bettered.

This sportsman of charm and intelligence reached the climax of his career by winning the gold medal at Sydney, his third Olympic appearance. He entered the arena carrying a tin of sardines – a symbol, he said, of the parable of the loaves and fishes with which Jesus fed the 5,000. Throughout his distinguished athletics career, Edwards attested 'God comes first in my life'. Until 1993 he refused to compete on a Sunday, thus missing out on an almost certain gold medal at the 1991 World Championships.

Edwards was voted British Sportsman of the Year, BBC Sports Personality of the Year and the IAAF Athlete of the Year in 1995, British Male Athlete of the Year in 1995, 2000 and 2001, and received the MBE in 1995 and the CBE in 2001. In 2003, having become one of only a handful of athletes to hold all four major titles at the same time – Olympic, World, European and Commonwealth – Edwards retired. The media career which followed has been equally distinguished. For many years he hosted the BBC's *Songs of Praise*, has presented a documentary on St Paul, and is a regular pundit and commentator for radio and television. In addition, he holds honorary doctorates from the Universities of Exeter and Ulster, and is a graduate in Physics from Durham.

With his high profile and evangelising, it was inevitable that the media should make much of Edwards' sudden and public loss of faith in 2007, when he gave up presenting *Songs of Praise*. He told *The Times* that 'when you think about it rationally, it does seem incredibly improbable that there is a God'.

Edwards was an ambassador for the London 2012 bid and has been appointed the athlete member on the London Organising Committee for the Olympic Games, the unanimous choice of the British Athletes Commission.

Darren Campbell
2004 Athens
Athletics, 4x100m Relay

Darren Campbell was one of the world's finest sprinters in his day, having won more than 21 medals, including Olympic gold and silver, Commonwealth and World Championship bronze and seven national titles. Twice denied medals by his teammate's drug-taking, he finally achieved his ambition of Olympic gold in the 4x100m relay in 2004.

Growing up in a tough environment in Manchester, Campbell was equally talented at athletics and football. As an athlete, he competed in 100m, 200m and 4x100m relay, winning medals at the English Schools, European Junior and World Junior Championships. He spent much of 1993 in Australia training with Linford Christie and made his senior international debut in the 4x100m race at the Stuttgart World Championships in 1993, but shortly afterwards he returned to his other love, soccer. The decision to switch was made largely because of peer pressure to take drugs: having been injured in a car accident, one of the medical team treating him suggested he needed to 'get on the juice'. Disillusioned by the widespread use of drugs

in athletics he turned his back on it, took a job with an insurance company and played semi-pro football, including for Plymouth Argyle, Weymouth and Newport County.

In 1995, Campbell felt the urge to return to sprinting, and by 1996 had his time for the 100m down to 10.17 seconds. His first appearance at the Olympic Games in 1996 proved a disaster when the baton was dropped in the relay and the British team eliminated. In 2000, he was back for the Sydney Olympics, where he came sixth in the 100m final, and took a surprise silver medal in the 200m, his first senior medal at that distance. Even in Sydney the spectre of drugs pursued him when he was offered growth hormones. He refused, of course, and when asked why he hadn't reported it to the authorities, said: 'Who would believe a black kid from Moss Side, who'd been surrounded by drugs most of his life?'

A hamstring injury (and difficulties in his home life which drove him close to suicide) kept Campbell off the track for much of 2001, but in 2002 he returned to fitness to run in the 100m and 4x100m relay at the European

Darren Campbell, looking relaxed as he runs in the heats of the 200m race in Athens.

Championships. The event was marred by Dwaine Chambers' doping conviction; Campbell's bronze in the 100m sprint was thus upgraded to a silver, but he and the rest of the team were stripped of the gold medal in the relay. In 2003 at the World Championships, he was to lose another medal because of Chambers' drug-taking, again in the 4x100m relay, although he won bronze in the 100m. In Athens, the 4x100m relay team of Jason Gardener, Darren Campbell, Marlon Devonish and Mark Lewis-Francis secured Olympic gold for the first time in the event since 1912 (beating the American team by just 0.01), a medal for which Campbell had long striven so hard.

The years between 2004 and his retirement in 2006 netted Campbell one more gold medal, in the 4x100m relay at the 2006 European Championships in Gothenburg. In the British team was Dwaine Chambers, and Campbell caused something of a stir by leaving the track immediately after the event without joining his teammates for the lap of honour. This was apparently in protest at Chambers' drug record, and the resultant loss of two medals, as well as his refusal to name his suppliers. Campbell was criticised at the time, since his coach, Linford Christie, had also served a drugs ban: he defended himself by saying he believed Christie had been unjustly convicted. The whole issue has recently been reopened with the ruling by the Court of Arbitration for Sport that the BOA's lifetime ban of athletes for drugs offences is illegal – meaning that Dwaine Chambers could return to Team GB for the 2012 Olympics. Campbell, though he has no personal animosity to Chambers, has been vociferous in his opposition to the decision to allow 'cheats' back into competition.

A man of passion and high principles ('I only fear my Mum and God'), Campbell was awarded the MBE in 2005 for his services to sport. He retired in 2006, and the following year was appointed the ambassador for Sky Sports Living for Sport, an initiative to involve young potential dropouts in sport, in which role he has proved an inspiration. He was part of the BBC's Radio 5 Live commentary team for the 2008 Beijing Olympics.

Campbell has also made a name for himself in other sporting circles, coaching Premier League football teams and Premiership rugby teams, and running training sessions. As an expert on pace and acceleration, his advice is highly valued. Campbell owns a professional sports supplement company, and has been a Special Olympics Great Britain Ambassador since 2007. As an adoptive Welshman (and with three children who are half-Welsh), in 2012 he was invited to join Sport Wales's initiative to achieve medal success at the 2014 Commonwealth Games.

Marlon Devonish

2004 Athens
Athletics, 4x100m Relay

Marlon Devonish has become one of the world's most decorated sprinters, with a total of nine gold medals at senior level, as well as one silver and four bronzes – an outstanding record which has earned him the nickname 'the Legend'. He's also one of the genuinely nice guys of athletics. At the British Championships in 2006, he became the first man since Linford Christie in 1988 to win both the 100m and 200m races at that event.

The young Devonish excelled at football, tennis and basketball at school in Coventry, and at the age of 16 took up running. This was a late age to start a career in sprinting, but within less than a year he had begun winning races. He became English Schools champion at 200m in 1994 and 100m in 1995, and won double gold at the 1995 European Junior Championships.

2002 was a great year for the sprinter. Having

Marlon Devonish punches the air after winning the 200m final at the 2003 IAAF World Indoor Championships.

won the European Cup 200m, he went on to win a silver medal in the 200m and a gold medal in the 4x100m relay at the Commonwealth Games in front of an enthusiastic home crowd in Manchester. The following year saw him win a third 200m gold medal in the World Indoor Championships.

But perhaps his finest performance was at the 2004 Athens Olympics, where Great Britain defeated the favourites, the USA, in the final of the 4x100m relay by a photo-finish one hundredth of a second – a particularly sweet victory since he had lost his silver medal in the 2003 World Championships when Dwaine Chambers tested positive for drugs after the team finished second. In recognition of his achievements Devonish was awarded the MBE in 2004.

In 2006 Devonish won a European Championship gold in the 4x100m relay and took bronze in the 200m.

His second appearance at the Olympics in 2008 was something of a disappointment: he failed to make the final in the 200m individual event and the 4x100m relay team was disqualified in the heats after Craig Pickering failed to pass the baton to Devonish on the final leg.

After a disappointing early 2010 season, another gold medal came with the 4x100 relay at the Commonwealth Games in Delhi. Plagued with injury during 2011, Devonish contemplated retiring, but a good showing at the World Championships in South Korea (where he made the finals of the 100m and the 4x100m relay – an achievement considering he was up against a certain Usain Bolt) put that out of his mind.

Devonish will be 36 in 2012, but is still a force to be recokoned with, and the thought of competing in a third Olympic Games, this time on home turf, has made him determined to end his career in style with a medal at the 2012 London Games.

When not training and racing, he devotes himself to his other passion, art, and has made quite a name for himself in this field.

'Too nice to run,' they said. Rubbish!

Chris Hoy
2004 Athens and 2008 Beijing
Cycling, 1km Time Trial (2004), Sprint (2008), Team Sprint (2008) & Keirin (2008)

Born in Edinburgh in 1976, Chris Hoy is already a legend. Dubbed by the press as 'the flying Scotsman' and 'the real McHoy' he is his country's most successful Olympian, the first Briton for a century to win three gold medals at the same Games, and the most successful Olympic male cyclist in history. Add to this a silver medal in international rowing, a degree in Applied Sports Science, three honorary doctorates and a knighthood, then throw in good looks and an engaging personality, and you have a true sporting hero.

The only man to have won a world and Olympic title in four different track disciplines and the holder of ten World Championship titles, Hoy's historic success at the Beijing Games rocketed him to international fame and into the hearts of the British nation. His Olympic career began in Sydney in 2000, when he won a silver medal in the team sprint, and four years later in Athens he took gold in the 1km time trial.

This event was then dropped from the Olympics, to make way for the BMX competition, a sport in which Hoy excelled as a boy. But he turned his attention to the keirin event which replaced the 'Kilo'. The keirin involves riders following a small motorbike or 'derny' around a 250m track. Having built up speed and with 2.5 of the nine laps to go, the derny pulls off and the riders race like fury to the finish. By 2008, Hoy was already the two-time world champion in this discipline, and to no one's surprise took the gold medal at the Beijing Games. Gold medals in the team sprint and individual sprint gave him the historic hat-trick.

A serious hip injury sustained in early 2009 when he crashed out during the Copenhagen World Cup keirin final put Hoy out of action for ten weeks, and prevented him defending his keirin and sprint titles at the World Championships in Poland.

He returned to form in August 2009 at the Fenioux Trophy in France – a prestigious competition comprising three sprint events, of which he won two and took the overall title. Hoy's impressive form continued in October, when he won three gold medals in Manchester at the first round of the 2009/10 World Cup series.

A popular and distinguished sportsman even before Beijing, Hoy was named Scottish Sports Personality of the Year in 2003 and was awarded an MBE in 2005. Three years later, after returning from Beijing in triumph, he was named Sportsman of the Year by the Sports Journalists' Association of Great Britain, and voted the 2008 BBC Sports Personality of the Year. He was awarded a knighthood in the 2009 New Year Honours List and his mother Carol received an MBE in the same list for services to healthcare.

With 2012 in mind, he opted to attend the European Track Championships in November 2010, rather than the Commonwealth Games in Delhi, but was surprisingly eliminated in the individual sprint. But in December 2010, he left

Chris Hoy celebrates his win in the sprint final at the Laoshan Velodrome in Beijing.

nothing to chance and won the gold medal in the keirin at the Melbourne World Cup.

In the various cycling disciplines he has mastered, Hoy has been 11 times World Champion, twice Commonwealth Champion, and has won 31 World Cup gold medals, ten silver and four bronze. He holds the records for the Olympic 200m TT and Kilo and the Commonwealth Games Kilo and Team Sprint – and he shows no sign of stopping.

Hoy's eleventh World title, in the keirin event, came in Melbourne in April 2012. On the last corner, Hoy was boxed in and, in an uncharacteristic manoeuvre he says was instinctive, went for a gap that wasn't really there, scraping through and beating the German Maximilian Levy by two one-hundredths of a second.

Hoy's talents have not always been confined to the cycle track. As a boy he was a talented rugby player, and was a British junior champion rower. Perhaps neither of these sports were enough to fuel his passion for speed. He has flown an RAF fighter jet, he races cars (and owns a Lotus 2-Eleven track car which can do 0-60mph in 3.8 seconds!). But on a cycle, the speed generated by his own enormous 'oak-sized' thighs, he is peerless, clocking a top speed of 48.8mph.

As the London Games approach, British Cycling has a supremely powerful team. Cycling is, after all, our strongest Olympic sport. Changes (extremely confusing ones until recently) have been made to the rules regarding nation and rider quotas, but Britain will be fielding the maximum – eight men and six women. Sir Chris looks a strong possibility for the team sprint, the keirin and the individual sprint, and there will be few more popular winners in 2012.

Kelly Holmes
2004 Athens
Athletics, 800m & 1,500m

Kelly Holmes is probably the finest female middle-distance runner Britain has ever produced. At the Athens Olympics of 2004 she overcame injury and depression to race into the record books, becoming the first British woman to win two Olympic track gold medals, the first athlete to do so at the same Games since 1920, and only the third woman in history to achieve the 800m and 1,500m double, setting a new

British record in the latter. An outstandingly popular winner, she returned home to an ecstatic reception. More than 40,000 people turned out to greet her in her home town of Tonbridge in Kent. She was made an MBE in recognition of her achievement, as well as being awarded the BBC Sports Personality of the Year.

Dogged by injury which affected seven of her 12 years of top-class competition, she nonetheless appeared in three Olympic Games, taking the two memorable gold medals as well as a bronze, and won medals in numerous World, Commonwealth and European championships. The guts and determination needed to overcome the repeated setbacks of fractures, ruptured tendons, torn calf muscles and viruses, not to mention the clinical depression which reduced her to self-harm and near suicide, have been a hallmark of her personality and endeared her to millions.

Born in Kent, the daughter of a Jamaican-born car mechanic and an English mother, Holmes had a troubled childhood. She began training for athletics when she was 12 and in only her second season won the English schools 1,500m title. Watching Sebastian Coe winning the 1,500m in Los Angeles put dreams of Olympic gold medals in her head. At 18, she joined the British Army, initially as a lorry driver and later as a PT

Eyes popping with delight, Kelly Holmes celebrates her win in the 800m race in Athens in 2004.

instructor. She became the Army judo champion, won the heptathlon, and even competed in the men's 800m on one occasion, since she was considered too powerful a runner to compete in the women's race without humiliating the others. Again, it was Olympics, this time the 1992 Games, that inspired her and she returned to international athletics, until 1997 combining her Army and athletics careers.

In 2005 Kelly was created a DBE, and in August she entered her final race in the UK, the 800m at the Norwich Union British Grand Prix, but suffered a recurrence of the Achilles tendon injury and finished only eighth. This final lap of honour of her career had to be completed by buggy, and at the end of that year she announced her retirement. Though no longer competing, she remains a popular figure and one of Britain's most recognisable sportswomen, appearing regularly on television in such diverse programmes as BBC London News (as sports presenter), ITV's *Dancing on Ice* and Channel 5's *Superstars*.

She continues working for charity, as she has done throughout her career, and has set up the DKH Legacy Trust which harnesses the talents of retired athletes to help the less fortunate. In May 2009 she was named president of Commonwealth Games England, succeeding Sir Christopher Chataway.

Along with Matthew Pinsent, Jayne Torvill and Christopher Dean, Dame Kelly has joined the Olympic Athletes Hub, which aims to increase engagement between Olympic fans and athletes at the 2012 Games.

Bradley Wiggins

2004 Athens and 2008 Beijing
Cycling, Individual Pursuit (2004 & 2008), Team Pursuit (2008)

'It's only bloody sport,' said Bradley Wiggins in Athens, having just become the first Briton for 40 years to win three Olympic medals at a single Games. In 2008 he won the individual pursuit gold medal in Beijing, a second gold in the team pursuit, and with his bronze medal from the 2000 Sydney Games took his Olympic tally to seven medals.

His successes in Athens came in the individual pursuit, the team pursuit and the Madison – a somewhat curious 50km event in which two riders work together to score points in a series of sprints every 20 laps, each sprint kicked off by a 'hand sling' as they take turns to propel each other into action. Halfway through the final, Wiggins' partner, Rob Hayles, crashed out and it looked like their medal chance was gone. But Hayles remounted and they fought back to take the bronze.

At Beijing he became the first ever rider successfully to defend a pursuit title, and with the pursuit team was instrumental in breaking the world record in the heats, and again in the final.

Wiggins' father was a professional cyclist, racing in Belgium where Bradley was born. (He scarpered when his son was just a boy, turned to drink and died in Australia in 2008). Though tall for a cyclist at 6'3", 'Wiggo' proved a natural in the saddle, winning his first race as a 12-year-old. At 18, he won the world junior pursuit title. At 20, Wiggins turned professional and signed for team Linda McCartney, and his career suffered a brief blip as the team disintegrated after internal squabbles. He joined the French team Française des Jeux and resumed his journey to the top of his sport, first with them, then with Crédit Agricole, Cofidis, and the highly successful Garmin-Slipstream.

In July 2009, with close to a million people crowding the slopes of Mont Ventoux to watch the final mountain stage of the Tour de France, Wiggins clung on determinedly to his fourth place to become only the second Briton in a century to finish in the top four. He had shed 7kg before the event as he changed his focus from track to road racing. The 2010 Tour was not such a happy event, however, and as part of the new Team Sky, he could manage only 24th place. The failure was 'a humbling experience'. That, and the death of his beloved grandfather shortly after, have, he says, given him a new perspective on life.

He entered the Tour again in 2011, but crashed out with a broken collarbone after stage 7, but is undaunted and will ride again in 2012, even though the Tour takes place so close to the Olympics. At the end of 2011, Wiggins won yet another medal, the silver in the UCI Road World Championships Time Trial.

Wiggins has won medals at every World Championships from 1998 to 2009 (seven of them gold, three of them at the same event in 2008), two silver medals at the Commonwealth

'Wiggo', draped in the Union Flag, waves to fans after winning the individual track pursuit in 2004.

Games, in the prologue of the Tour de France, and many other stages of international road races.

Wiggins was awarded the OBE in 2005 and became a CBE in 2009. His autobiography, *In Pursuit of Glory*, was published in 2008.

Talented, dedicated and supremely hardworking, Wiggins is laid-back about his status as a cycling superstar and inspirational hero: '. . . it's actually clear and simple. It's just a case of going from point A to B as fast as you can.

Why be overawed by the occasion, just because you've got a chance to win the opening stage of the world's biggest race or because three million people are watching on television?'

The 2012 season started well for Wiggins, when he came first overall in the Paris-Nice and, in April, the Tour de Romandie (the first British rider to do so). But the changes to the cycling programme for the 2012 Games are not good news for Wiggins, as the men's individual pursuit has been dropped in the interests of giving men and women parity in the events open to them. 'It's a shame,' he said, 'it will probably end up killing off track endurance cycling.'

Nonetheless, Wiggins can still make history by winning the Tour de France.

Rebecca Adlington
2008 Beijing
Swimming, 400m Freestyle & 800m Freestyle

At the age of 19, Adlington swam into the record books and to international fame by becoming only the second woman to win two gold medals at the same Games for 100 years. In the 800m heats, she set a new British, Commonwealth, European and Olympic record of 8:18.06, and in the final broke the world record with a time of 8:14.10. She also broke the Commonwealth record in the 400m heats with a time of 4:02.24. To add to her two gold medals, Adlington swam the final leg of the 4x200m relay and won the bronze.

Adlington began swimming at the age of four, and was competing at the age of ten. She trains at the local Sherwood Swimming Baths in Mansfield, Nottinghamshire, which has been renamed in her honour. Defeat in the 2007 World Championships saw her leave the pool in tears after failing to make the final. Spurred on by this setback, she began a punishing training schedule, rising at 5 a.m., swimming 8,000m a day, running and circuit training. 'It's all sleeping,

Adlington watches the scoreboard and sees that she has broken the 800m freesytyle world record in Beijing.

training, driving and occasionally finding time to eat. That's what my life is about,' she said. The hard work paid off: she qualified for the Olympic 200m, 400m and 800m freestyle events.

Adlington returned from Beijing to a heroine's welcome in her home town of Mansfield. An overnight star, she has become known not only for her prodigious talent, but for her love of shoes. Her mother's reward to her for qualifying for the British Olympic team was a £275 pair of Christian Louboutin shoes.

She was made an OBE in 2008 as well as being named the Sports Journalists' Association Sportswoman of the Year. The pressure of adulation and expectation took some adjusting to, but Adlington is nothing if not single-mindedly determined.

When the new go-faster 100 percent polyurethane swimsuits were launched on the market in 2009, most of her fellow competitors enthusiastically adopted them. The governing body of the sport, FINA, initially banned them, but had to lift the ban after threats of lawsuits. A similar storm had greeted the introduction of the Speedo LZR suit (which Adlington wears) two years previously. Since the new suits reduce drag and provide buoyancy some consider they confer unfair advantage and constitute a form of cheating. Adlington called it 'technological doping' and was adamant that she would not switch. 'I would never in a million years take a drug to help me, so why would I wear a suit just to improve my performance?' Though criticised in some quarters at the time, she was vindicated by FINA's decision in the summer of 2009 to ban all full-body super-suits.

In November 2010 at the Commonwealth Games in Delhi, Adlington added two more gold medals to her tally, in the 400m and 800m freestyle, and two bronzes in the 200m freestyle and 4x200m freestyle. In 2011 she was British champion over 200m, 400m and 800m. To nobody's surprise, in March 2012 Adlington qualified in style for Team GB's Olympic squad with a win in the 800m at the British Gas Championships.

Adlington plans to add the 200m and 4x200m relay to her gold medal winning distances for the 2012 London Olympics, and British hopes will be riding on her.

Victoria Pendleton
2008 Beijing
Cycling, Sprint

Victoria Pendleton is not just a pretty face, she is Britain's most successful woman cyclist, the winner of an Olympic gold medal and 13 World Championship medals (six of them gold), and is the reigning British, Commonwealth, World and Olympic sprint champion. Anyway, to call her pretty would be an understatement. In a sport where short limbs and huge muscles are the norm, Pendleton is lithe and tall, and glamorous – though not short of muscle: 'I'm proud of my thighs. They're the tools of my trade,' she says. When she returned from Beijing with the gold medal, the media went wild for interviews, photoshoots and public appearances – more than for all the other Olympic victors put together – and sponsors and TV shows courted her. Since then she has appeared on numerous magazine covers, in advertising and marketing campaigns and famously posed naked on her cycle for *Observer Sport Monthly*.

Pendleton's father was a British national grass track cycling champion and encouraged his three children to take up the sport at a very early age. Victoria and her twin brother began competing at the age of nine on local grass tracks in Bedfordshire. Although spotted as a promising talent at the age of 16 and invited to Manchester for national trials, she decided to concentrate on her education. Nonetheless, the trial gave her a taste for indoor track cycling and she competed when her studies allowed. On graduating from Northumbria University in 2002 she became a full-time cyclist.

Though showing great promise in competing in the European Championships and Commonwealth Games, success in the sprint eluded her, and she became frustrated. Chosen for the squad for the 2004 Athens Games, it looked like her hour had come, but she froze and could only manage sixth place. She was devastated, cried for days and considered giving up the sport for ever.

Working with the British team's psychiatrist, Steve Peters, she gradually succeeded in renewing her self-belief, drive and commitment

to cycling. In March 2005 she won her first World Championship sprint title in Los Angeles. She followed this with World Cup and Commonwealth Games wins in 2006, but lost the world title later in Bordeaux.

Teaming up with a new coach, Jan van Eijden, in 2007 seemed to provide a formidable boost to

A delighted Victoria Pendleton wins the sprint title in Beijing in 2008.

her confidence and she won three gold medals at the World Championships that year, as well as being awarded the *Sunday Times* Sportswoman of the Year award. In the build-up to the 2008 Games, Pendleton won two more gold medals and a silver at the Track World Championships.

And there in Beijing, to no one's surprise, she won the gold medal. Together with the rest of the British Olympians, she was invited to a reception at Buckingham Palace, and later in the year received the MBE.

At the 2009 World Championships, Pendleton again won the World Track sprint title, and in 2010 made it five titles in six years. At the British National Track Championships in both 2009 and 2010 she yet again took the sprint and keirin titles, as well as the 500m time trial in 2010. (For those who have lost count, that made a total of nine successive national sprint titles.)

In 2011 she managed only third place in the individual sprint World Championships, but was back in winning form in 2012 to win her sixth individual sprint crown. Although this event made her the equal most successful female track cyclist of all time with Galina Zareva of the Soviet Union, the event was anything but comfortable for her.

In the semi-finals she was up against arch-rival and defending champion Anna Meares of Australia. It was best-of-three and in the first race the two collided; Pendleton crashed heavily and was relegated. In the second race, Meares was similarly relegated for not holding her line, and in the deciding race Pendleton, bruised and track-burned with her skinsuit half-shredded, squeaked home to qualify for the finals, which she won 2-0. The two are likely to meet in the final of the London Games, and what a race that would be.

In December 2009 the IOC ratified the changes to the 2012 cycling programme, to give men and women parity with five events each – sprint, keirin, team sprint, team pursuit and omnium. This means that Victoria Pendleton has every chance of emulating Sir Chris Hoy's achievement of three gold medals at a single Games.

Tim Brabants
2008 Beijing
K-1 (Kayak Single), 1,000m

Even Tim Brabants' greatest rival, Paul Wycherly, admits that he is 'the best 1,000m paddler in the world'. Indeed, Brabants has a list of major wins as long as one of his very muscular arms. He is the current Olympic K-1 1,000m champion – the first ever British gold medallist in the sport – and is a multiple World and European champion.

Having taken up canoeing at the age of ten, Brabants first competed in the Olympics in 2000 at Sydney, where he won a bronze medal in the K-1 1,000m, then competed in the Athens Games in 2004 where, in spite of qualifying for the final with a world record of 3:24.412, he finished a disappointing fifth.

At the Beijing Games, Brabants fulfilled his ambition by winning gold in the K-1 1,000m, and winning it in style by leading all the way. Three days later he also took bronze in the 500m.

Although known as a sprinter, Brabants' first success at senior level was in the marathon in 1997.

A doctor by profession, Brabants has his work cut out combining his athletic career with his medical duties. Having qualified at Nottingham University in 2002, he has put his medical career on hold more than once to concentrate on training for the Olympics. Now, in 2012, his A&E duties are on hold again as he prepares for the home Games.

Since winning the Junior World Championships (K-2) in 1995, Brabants has notched up an impressive number of wins in all the sport's

Tim Brabants paddling his way to a gold medal in Beijing.

major competitions, including the 1,000m K-1 European Championships in 2002, 2006, 2007 and 2008, and the World Cup in 2007 and 2008.

The year 2011 was not his best, largely due to an injury which kept him out of training for many months. In the 2011 World Championships he teamed up with Ben Farrell in the K-2, but they failed to make the medals.

Three months' training in South Africa has seen him return to form, fitter and stronger than ever, and with a good chance of selection for the 2012 Games. On returning to the UK in May (leaving his South African-born wife and baby daughter behind temporarily) he took part in the first of three selections for the K-1 1,000m place in 2012. He won – by three-hundredths of a second ahead of Paul Wycherly! The boat itself has already qualified, thanks to GB being the host nation, but the paddler is still to be decided. By the time you read this, chances are that the paddler will be Brabants.

Like many other athletes in the Spring of 2012, Brabants has loudly deplored the ruling by the Court of Arbitration for Sport that the BOA's lifetime ban of athletes for drugs offences is illegal, and the consequent possibility of Dwaine Chambers returning to Team GB for the 2012 Olympics.

It's no wonder he has strong feelings on the subject. Back in 2000, the man who beat Brabants into third place was the Bulgarian Petar Merkov, who had failed a doping test just before the Games (though the Bulgarian denied it). 'Who knows what was going on in 2000? I was happy with the bronze at the time, but that's an Olympic silver medal I'll never have,' said Brabants.

Christine Ohuruogu
2008 Beijing
Athletics, 400m

Christine Ohuruogu, the first British female 400m Olympic champion, is a superb athlete and no stranger to controversy. She went from being the Golden Girl and media darling in Beijing to vilification by all and sundry when banned from competing for missing three drugs tests, then becoming the 'forgotten woman of British athletics', and now, on the verge of the 2012 Games, has re-emerged into the limelight as a serious hope for Team GB's medal chances.

One of eight children born in Newham, East London (a stone's throw from the Olympic Stadium in Stratford) to Igbo Nigerian parents, Ohuruogu was a bright and athletic child. While at University College London she played netball (for England in the U17 and U19) and took up athletics seriously, specialising in the 400m. A bronze medallist at the European Junior Championships, and an AAA 400m champion, she was in the squad for the 2004 Olympics in Athens for the 400m and the 4x400m relay (making the semi-finals in the former and coming fourth in the latter). She followed this with a bronze medal in the relay at the 2005 World Championships, finding time during training and competition to achieve a degree in Linguistics (with a thesis on swear words).

The following year started well: a gold in the 400m at the Commonwealth Games, with a personal best time, and there should have been another gold in the relay, but for an unfortunate mix-up with the lanes and baton change which saw the team relegated to silver. Then it all started to go wrong.

Having just run a 'crap' race at Crystal Palace in July 2006 (coming last), Ohuruogu was accosted by the head of UK Athletics and a bevy of officials. She had missed three out-of-competition drugs tests and suddenly found herself slapped with a year's ban by the International Association of Athletics Federations, and threatened with a lifetime ban by the British Olympic Association. The rules require athletes to submit their training schedules to the authorities, offering five one-hour slots of their own choosing in order to be tested, and Ohuruogu later admitted to 'bad time management'. She missed the first appointment (we're not sure why, but that was forgivable), the second because she forgot and was busy writing an article (silly and serious) and the third after she got lost on the A12 (automatic ban). There was never any suggestion that she *had* taken drugs*, but rules is rules. When the BOA wanted to ban her for life, she was devastated and angry and (as she said) 'threatened hell and destruction'. There followed a long, expensive – and successful – battle to have the decision overturned.

---

* One of the most entertaining excuses for failing a drugs test came from French tennis player Richard Gasquet, who said the cocaine found in his system during the Sony Ericsson Open in Florida had entered his body through the mouth of a woman he kissed in a nightclub! He got away with it.

But Ohuruogu is nothing if not resilient and she shook off the constant barrage of adverse press coverage. The criticism was more wounding for her family than herself: she declared that she didn't give a damn what people thought of her and used the time out to have an operation on her Achilles tendon. She returned to competition in fine form at the World Athletics Championships in Osaka, which began shortly after the completion of her ban. Passing the finishing line millimetres ahead of the field, she pulled up, bent double, looked up at the cameras and said with a big smile, 'Was it me?' It was the only gold the British team won

at the championships, though the relay team took the bronze.

But the press were still hammering away. *The Sun* newpaper ranted, 'We can't let Ohuruogu be the face of 2012', in reference to the star's proposed billing as the poster girl of London 2012, accusing her of arrogance, feeble excuses and lack of contrition.

Then came Beijing, the race of her life (where she came from fifth to first in the last 100 metres), the gold medal and an MBE.

A hamstring problem in 2009 and a season with only one win led to an indifferent season in 2010, including her withdrawal from the Commonwealth Games, and a disqualification in the World Championships the following year in Daegu, South Korea, for false-starting.

Four years without a world title, but come 2012 and Ohuruogu is very much back on track. Shaking off the injuries, the press hostility and the false-start, she stormed back into Olympic form at the World Indoor Championships in Istanbul in March, winning the gold medal in the 4x400m relay with Shana Cox, Nicola Sanders and Perri Shakes-Drayton. Running the third leg, she took the baton 10 metres behind the American race leader, and handed it on three metres ahead of her.

She was back to being the 'Golden Girl' in *The Sun*'s eyes (no hard feelings there, then!), and very much in contention for another Olympic gold. And watch out for her younger sister, Victoria, a budding sprint star.

The trademark beaming smile lights up on Christine Ohuruogu's face after winning the gold medal in the 400m in Beijing in 2008.

Glorious Failures, Unlucky Losers and Other Oddities

A book on British Olympic greats would not be complete without some mention of those unfortunates who should have won but didn't and those who gloriously, heroically and memorably failed in their endeavours.

Eddie 'the Eagle' Edwards, the buffoonish, bespectacled, bulky plasterer from Cheltenham, is Britain's – if not the world's – favourite failure. Coming last in the 70m and 90m ski jump competitions at the 1988 Winter Games in Calgary, he captured the hearts of millions. The worse he did, the more they loved him. As the world watched, unsure whether it was bravery or idiocy they were witnessing and convinced that he was leaping to his death, Eddie twice launched himself into space, arms flailing and half-blind, and . . . survived on landing.

A mere two years before the Games, Eddie had developed an urge to compete in the Olympics and reckoned that since there were no other British entrants in the ski jumping, here lay his chance. A self-taught skier, he had never jumped, had no kit, and no funding,

Eddie Edwards, soaring like an eagle, launches himself into last place in the 70m ski jump in Calgary and into the hearts of millions.

and when he eventually decided to take lessons from the experts most of it went over his head since he didn't speak French or German. He was overweight and needed thick glasses to see where he was going. Arriving in Canada, his luggage burst open on the airport carousel, damaging his ski bindings. He managed only one practice jump, got locked out of his cabin and was refused entry to his own press conference because he didn't have his credentials on him.

The Olympic officials were not amused and thought Eddie was taking the mickey. But his personality, wit and sheer guts won them round in the end. In his closing speech, the President of the Games said, 'At this Olympic Games some competitors have won gold and some have broken records, and one has even flown like an eagle'. It was the only time in Olympic history that an individual has been thus singled out, and the 100,000-strong audience roared, 'Ed*deee! Eddeee!*'

But however endearing he was, the IOC determined that there should be no repeat of this clownish performance and instigated the 'Eddie the Eagle rule', by which Olympic hopefuls are required to compete in international events and be in the top 30 percent of competitors. Thus ended Eddie's further Olympic dreams. He returned to plastering but did, however, make a successful sideline out of media appearances and afterdinner speaking, wrote his autobiography, and went on to study law.

Not many remember who won in 1988, but everyone remembers Eddie.

It was 1908, the Olympic venue was London, and **Philip Plater** of Great Britain became the Olympic small-bore rifle champion that never was. In fading light, wind and drizzle, with only half an hour to go before the time limit, Plater fired 80 rounds, setting a new world record of 391. He was declared the winner. A day later it emerged that he was not officially entered in the 12-man competition, after a disastrous mix-up by the British team officials. The entry forms for one of the squad, George Barnes, had been lost and Plater was put down as 12th man. Barnes' entry form was then discovered, he was awarded the bronze medal and the unfortunate Plater's superb effort was discounted.

Perhaps it was some consolation to him to receive a gold medal and a diploma from the British Olympic Council, but his name will never show up in the official Olympic records as gold medallist.

British fencer **Judy Guinness** (full name Heather Seymour Guinness Penn-Hughes) was another who was denied a gold medal, all because of her sporting nature and sense of fair play.

At the 1932 Los Angeles Games the scores showed that she had beaten her opponent, Ellen Preis of Austria, in the final. Guinness pointed out to the officials that they had failed to spot two of Preis' touches. This sportsmanship, embodying the true spirit of the Olympic movement, meant she returned home with only a silver medal.

In 1948, four happy Britons stood on the podium, received their gold medals for the 4x100m relay and heard their national anthem ring out. The Americans had beaten them to the finish, but were disqualified for a baton passing infringement. But hardly had the Brits had time to admire their medals before the verdict was reversed after a review of the race footage, and they reluctantly swapped gold for silver.

And spare a thought for **Lorna Johnstone** who attended three Olympic Games and, six months short of her 70th birthday, came fifth in the mixed dressage team equestrian event in 1972. Fifth place may also have been second-to-last, but she has entered the record books as the oldest British Olympic competitor. The oldest ever Olympian is Oscar Swahn of Sweden, who won three gold medals, two bronze and a silver for shooting deer (well, deer-shaped targets) at the age of almost 73.

While we are straying from the point, here are a few more curiosities...

Whatever happened to the little lad who was in the winning boat of the coxed pairs in 1900? At the last minute, the Dutch jettisoned the 29-year-old doctor who had coxed them in the heat and installed a young French boy half his weight and less than half his age. After his 15 minutes of fame he became no more than a footnote in IOC records and no one even knows his name.

In 1900 the shooting events included live pigeons. It was a messy affair by all accounts. American sports historian Andrew Strunk described it thus in 1988: 'Maimed birds were writhing on the ground, blood and feathers were swirling in the air and women with parasols were weeping in the chairs set up nearby.'

That event was the only time medals were awarded for killing a live creature and was won by a Belgian.

Another somewhat absurd event held only in 1900, was the long jump for horses. It was won by another Belgian, but the horse, Extra Dry, was British through and through. Even so, it failed to clear anything like the distance achieved by human Olympians.

The 1992 Games featured an even more pointless event – solo synchronised swimming.

Few people have heard of **Lillian Board,** who could have been, should have been an Olympic gold medallist. In Mexico City in 1968, at the age of 19, she came achingly close to becoming the first British woman to win an Olympic 400m title, caught in the last few strides by the fast-finishing Colette Besson of France. The Munich Olympics of 1972 were approching and her time of glory nigh, but she died of cancer in a Munich clinic in December 1970, at just 22 years old.

A recent article in *The Times* highlighted the story of a Polish-born Jew named Ben Helfgott who, as a weightlifter, competed in two Olympics (1956 and 1960) and would have competed in a third (1952) but for appendicitis. In all, he attended nine consecutive Games. A survivor of three Nazi concentration camps (in which most of his family perished), he took British citizenship, embraced the British way of life and in following the Olympic flame found renewed faith in his fellows.

Table of All British Gold Medallists

Abrahams, Harold	1924	Athletics, 100m
Adlington, Rebecca	2008	Swimming, 400m Freestyle
		Swimming, 800m Freestyle
Ahearne, Timothy	1908	Athletics, Triple Jump
Ainslie, Ben	2000	Sailing, Laser Class
	2004	Sailing, Finn Class
	2008	Sailing, Finn Class
Ainsworth-Davis, John	1920	Athletics, 4x400m Relay
Allhusen, Derek	1968	Equestrian, 3-Day Team
Altwegg, Jeannette	1952	Figure Skating
Amoore, Edward	1908	Shooting, Small-bore Rifle Team
Applegarth, William	1912	Athletics, 4x100m Relay
Archer, Alex	1936	Ice Hockey
Aspin, John	1908	Sailing, 12m Class
Astor, John Jacob, 1st Baron Astor of Hever	1908	Rackets, Men's Doubles
Atkin, Charles	1920	Field Hockey
Attrill, Louis	2000	Rowing, Coxed Eights
Ayton, Sarah	2004	Sailing, Yngling Class
	2008	Sailing, Yngling Class
Bacon, Stanley	1908	Wrestling, Middleweight Freestyle
Badcock, John	1932	Rowing, Coxless Fours
Bailey, Horace	1908	Football
Baillon, Louis	1908	Field Hockey
Barber, Paul	1988	Field Hockey
Barrett, Edward	1908	Tug-of-War
Barrett, Frederick	1920	Polo
Barrett, Herbert Roper	1908	Lawn Tennis, Men's Indoor Doubles
Barridge, J.E see Burridge		
Bartlett, Charles	1908	Cycling, 100km

Batchelor, Stephen	1988	Field Hockey
Beachcroft, C.B.K.	1900	Cricket
Beesly, Richard	1928	Rowing, Coxless Fours
Bellville, Miles	1936	Sailing, 6m Class
Bennett, Charles	1900	Athletics, 1,500m
	1900	Athletics, 5,000m Team
Bennett, John	1920	Field Hockey
Bentham, Isaac	1912	Water Polo
Beresford, Jack	1924	Rowing, Single Sculls
	1932	Rowing, Coxless Fours
	1936	Rowing, Double Sculls
Beresford, John	1900	Polo
Berry, Arthur	1908	Football
	1912	Football
Bevan, Edward	1928	Rowing, Coxless Fours
Bhaura, Kulbir Singh	1988	Field Hockey
Bignal-Rand, Mary see Rand, Mary		
Bingley, Norman	1908	Sailing, 7m Class
Birchell, Francis	1900	Cricket
Birkett, Arthur	1900	Cricket
Blackstaffe, Harry	1908	Rowing, Single Sculls
Boardman, Chris	1992	Cycling, Individual Pursuit
Boardman, Christopher	1936	Yachting, 6m Class
Boland, John Pius	1896	Lawn Tennis, Men's Singles
	1896	Lawn Tennis, Men's Doubles
Bond, Richard	1948	Sailing, Swallow Class
Borland, Jimmy	1936	Ice Hockey
Bowerman, Alfred	1900	Cricket
Brabants, Tim	2008	Canoeing, K-1 1,000m
Braithwaite, Bob	1968	Shooting, Trap
Brasher, Chris	1956	Athletics, 3,000m Steeplechase
Brebner, Ronald	1912	Football
Brenchley, Edgar	1936	Ice Hockey
Brown, Arthur	1936	Athletics, 4x400m Relay

Bruce, Charles Granville[2]	1924	Alpine & Mixed Alpinism (Reaching summit of Mt Everest 1922)
Bruce, Geoffrey[2]	1924	Alpine & Mixed Alpinism (Reaching summit of Mt Everest 1922)
Buchanan, John	1908	Sailing, 12m Class
Buckenham, Claude	1900	Football
Buckley, George	1900	Cricket
Bucknall, Henry	1908	Rowing, Coxed Eights
Budgett, Richard	1984	Rowing, Coxed Fours
Bugbee, Charles	1912	Water Polo
	1920	Water Polo
Bullen, Jane	1968	Equestrian, 3-Day Team
Bunten, James	1908	Sailing, 12m
Burchell, Francis	1900	Cricket
Burgess, Edgar	1912	Rowing, Coxed Eights
Burghley, Lord David George	1928	Athletics, 400m Hurdles
Burn, Thomas	1912	Football
Burnell, Charles	1908	Rowing, Coxed Eights
Burnell, Richard	1948	Rowing, Double Sculls
Burridge T.E. aka Barridge, J.E.	1900	Football
Bushnell, Bertie	1948	Rowing, Double Sculls
Butler, Guy	1920	Athletics, 4x400m Relay
Campbell, Charles (Sir C. R. Campbell, Bt)	1908	Sailing, 8m Class
Campbell, Colin	1920	Field Hockey
Campbell, Darren	2004	Athletics, 4x100m Relay
Canning, George	1920	Tug-of-War
Carnell, Arthur	1908	Shooting, Small-bore Rifle
Cassels, Harold	1920	Field Hockey
Cecil, David (6th Marquess of Exeter) see Burghley, Lord David		
Chalk, Alfred	1900	Football
Chapman, Frederick	1908	Football
Chappell, James	1936	Ice Hockey

Christian, Frederick	1900	Cricket
Christie, Linford	1992	Athletics, 100m
Clancy, Ed	2008	Cycling, Team Pursuit
Clift, Robert	1988	Field Hockey
Clive, Lewis	1932	Rowing, Coxless Pairs
Coales, William	1908	Athletics, 3-Mile Team
Cochrane, Blair	1908	Sailing, 8m Class
Coe, Sebastian (Baron Coe of Ranmore)	1980	Athletics, 1,500m
	1984	Athletics, 1,500m
Coe, Thomas	1900	Water Polo
Coleman, Robert	1920	Sailing, 7m Class
Coode, Ed	2004	Rowing, Coxless Fours
Cook, Steph	2000	Modern Pentathlon
Cooke, Harold	1920	Field Hockey
Cooke, Nicole	2008	Cycling, Road Race
Cooper, Charlotte 'Chattie'	1900	Lawn Tennis, Mixed Doubles
	1900	Lawn Tennis, Women's Singles
Cooper, Malcolm	1984	Shooting, 50m Rifle Three Positions
	1988	Shooting, 50m Rifle Three Positions
Corbett, Walter	1908	Football
Corner, Harry	1900	Cricket
Cornet, George	1908	Water Polo
	1912	Water Polo
Cousins, Robin	1980	Figure Skating
Coward, John	1936	Ice Hockey
Cracknell, James	2000	Rowing, Coxless Fours
	2004	Rowing, Coxless Fours
Crawford, Colin	1924	Alpine & Mixed Alpinism (Reaching summit of Mt Everest 1922)
Crawshaw, Robert[2]	1900	Water Polo
Crichton, Charles	1908	Sailing, 6m Class
Crockford, Eric	1920	Field Hockey
Cross, Martin	1984	Rowing, Coxed Fours
Crummack, Reginald	1920	Field Hockey
Cudmore, Collier	1908	Rowing, Coxless Fours

Cuming, Frederick	1900	Cricket
Currie, Lorne	1900	Sailing, ½-1 Ton Class
	1900	Sailing, Open Class
Curry, John	1976	Figure Skating
D'Arcy, Victor	1912	Athletics, 4x100m Relay
Dailley, Gordon	1936	Ice Hockey
Daly, Denis St. George	1900	Polo
Davey, John Gerald	1936	Ice Hockey
Davies, Chris	1972	Sailing, Flying Dutchman Class
Davies, Lynn	1964	Athletics, Long Jump
de Relwyskow, George	1908	Wrestling, Lightweight Freestyle
Deakin, Joseph	1908	Athletics, 3-Mile Team
Dean, Christopher	1984	Ice Dancing
Dean, William	1920	Water Polo
DeGale, James	2008	Boxing, Middleweight
Dennis, Simon	2000	Rowing, Coxed Eights
Derbyshire, John	1908	Swimming, 4x200m Freestyle Relay
Devonish, Marlon	2004	Athletics, 4x100m Relay
Dines, Joseph	1912	Football
Dixon, Charles	1912	Lawn Tennis, Indoor Mixed Doubles
Dixon, Richard	1908	Sailing, 7m Class
Dixon, The Hon. T. Robin (Earl of Glentoran)	1964	Bobsleigh, Two-man
Dod, William	1908	Archery, York Round
Dodds, Richard	1988	Field Hockey
Doherty, Lawrence	1900	Lawn Tennis, Men's Singles
	1900	Lawn Tennis, Men's Doubles
Doherty, Reginald	1900	Lawn Tennis, Men's Doubles
	1900	Lawn Tennis, Mixed Doubles
	1908	Lawn Tennis, Men's Doubles
Donne, William	1900	Cricket
Douglas, Johnny	1908	Boxing, Middleweight
Douglas, Rowley	2000	Rowing, Coxed Eights
Downes, Arthur	1908	Sailing, 12m Class

Downes, John Henry	1908	Sailing, 12m Class
Duke, H (John)[1]	1908	Tug-of-War
Dunlop, David	1908	Sailing, 12m Class
Easte, Peter	1908	Shooting, Team Trap
Eastlake-Smith, Gwendoline aka Gladys	1908	Lawn Tennis, Women's Indoor Singles
Edwards, Hugh	1932	Rowing, Coxless Pairs
	1932	Rowing, Coxless Fours
Edwards, Jonathan	2000	Athletics, Triple Jump
Eley, Charles	1924	Rowing, Coxless Fours
Elliot, Launceston	1896	Weightlifting, One-Handed Lift
Ellison, Adrian	1984	Rowing, Coxed Fours
Erhardt, Carl	1936	Ice Hockey
Etherington-Smith, Raymond	1908	Rowing, Coxed Eights
Exshaw, E. William	1900	Sailing, 2-3 Ton Class
Faulds, Richard	2000	Shooting, Double Trap
Faulkner, David	1988	Field Hockey
Fenning, John	1908	Rowing, Coxless Pairs
Field-Richards, John	1908	Motor Boats, Class B
Finnegan, Chris	1968	Boxing, Middleweight
Fleming, John	1908	Shooting, Small-bore Rifle Moving Target
Fleming, Philip	1912	Rowing, Coxed Eights
Fletcher, Jennie	1912	Swimming, 4x100m Freestyle
Forsyth, Charles	1908	Water Polo
Foster, James	1936	Ice Hockey
Foster, Tim	2000	Rowing, Coxless Fours
Foster, William	1908	Swimming, 4x200m Freestyle Relay
Fox, Jim	1976	Modern Pentathlon
Freeman, Harry	1908	Field Hockey
Garcia, Russell	1988	Field Hockey

Gardener, Jason	2004	Athletics, 4×100m Relay
Garton, Arthur	1912	Rowing, Coxed Eights
George, Roland	1932	Rowing, Coxless Fours
Gillan, James	1908	Rowing, Coxless Fours
	1912	Rowing, Coxed Eights
Gladstone, Sir Albert, 5th Baronet	1908	Rowing, Coxed Eights
Glen-Coats, Thomas	1908	Sailing, 12m Class
Godfree, Kitty	1920	Lawn Tennis, Ladies' Doubles
Goodfellow, Frederick	1908	Tug-of-War
Goodhew, Duncan	1980	Swimming, 100m Breaststroke
Goodison, Paul	2008	Sailing, Laser Class
Gordon-Watson, Mary	1972	Equestrian, 3-Day Team
Gore, Arthur	1908	Lawn Tennis, Men's Indoor Singles
	1908	Lawn Tennis, Men's Indoor Doubles
Gosling, William	1900	Football
Grace, Frederick	1908	Boxing, Lightweight
Green, Eric	1908	Field Hockey
Green, Thomas	1932	Athletics, 50km Walk
Gretton, John (1st Baron Gretton)	1900	Sailing, ½-1 Ton Class
	1900	Sailing, Open Class
Griffiths, Cecil	1920	Athletics, 4×400m Relay
Grimley, Martin	1988	Field Hockey
Grinham, Judy	1956	Swimming, 100m Backstroke
Gruber, Luka	2000	Rowing, Coxed Eights
Gunn, Richard	1908	Boxing, Featherweight
Gunnell, Sally	1992	Athletics, 400m Hurdles
Halswelle, Wyndham	1908	Athletics, 400m
Hampson, Tommy	1932	Athletics, 800m
Hannam, Edith	1912	Lawn Tennis, Women's Indoor Singles
	1912	Lawn Tennis, Indoor Mixed Doubles
Hanney, Edward	1912	Football
Hardman, Harold	1908	Football
Harmer, Russell	1936	Yachting, 6m Class

Harrison, Audley	2000	Boxing, Super Heavyweight
Haslam, A.	1900	Football
Haslam, Harry	1920	Field Hockey
Hawkes, Robert	1908	Football
Hawtrey, Henry	1906[4]	Athletics, 5 miles
Hemery, David	1968	Athletics, 400m Hurdles
Henry, William	1900	Water Polo
Herbert, Garry	1992	Rowing, Coxed Pairs
Hill, Albert	1920	Athletics, 800m
	1920	Athletics, 1,500m
Hill, Arthur Edwin	1912	Water Polo
Hill, Bertie	1956	Equestrian, 3-Day Team
Hillyard, George	1908	Lawn Tennis, Men's Doubles
Hirons, William	1908	Tug-of-War
Hoare, Gordon	1912	Football
Hodge, Percy	1920	Athletics, 3,000m Steeplechase
Holman, Frederick	1908	Swimming, 200m Breaststroke
Holmes, Andy	1984	Rowing, Coxed Fours
	1988	Rowing, Coxless Fours
Holmes, Frederick	1920	Tug-of-War
Holmes, Dame Kelly	2000	Athletics, 800m
	2000	Athletics, 1,500m
Hope, Linton[1]	1900	Sailing, ½-1 Ton Class
	1900	Sailing, Open Class
Hore, Edward	1900	Sailing, 3-10 Ton Class
Horsfall, Ewart	1912	Rowing, Coxed Eights
Hoy, Sir Christopher	2004	Cycling, 1km Time Trial
	2008	Cycling, Team Sprint
	2008	Cycling, Sprint
	2008	Cycling, Keirin
Hughes, John	1932	Art, Town Planning
Humby, Harold	1908	Shooting, Small-bore Rifle Team
Humphreys, Frederick	1908	Tug-of-War
	1920	Tug-of-War
Hunt, Kenneth	1908	Football

Hunt-Davis, Ben	2000	Rowing, Coxed Eights
Hunter, Mark	2008	Rowing, Lightweight Double Sculls
Ireton, Albert	1908	Tug-of-War
Jackson, Arnold	1912	Athletics, 1,500m
Jackson, Laurence[2]	1924	Curling
Jackson, Willie[2]	1924	Curling
Jacobs, David	1912	Athletics, 4x100m Relay
James, Tom	2008	Rowing, Coxless Fours
Jarvis, John	1900	Swimming, 1,000m Freestyle
	1900	Swimming, 4,000m Freestyle
Jefferson, H. N.	1900	Sailing, 3-10 Ton Class
Johnson, Victor	1908	Cycling, 660 Yards
Johnstone, Banner	1908	Rowing, Coxed Eights
Jones, Ben	1968	Equestrian, 3-Day Team
Jones, Benjamin	1908	Cycling, 500m
	1908	Cycling, Team Pursuit
Jones, Christopher	1920	Water Polo
Jones, John.	1900	Football
Kelly, Frederick	1908	Rowing, Coxed Eights
Kemp, Peter	1900	Water Polo
Kenny, Jason	2008	Cycling, Team Sprint
Kerly, Sean	1988	Field Hockey
Kierly, Tom	1904	Athletics, Decathlon
Kilpatrick, Jack	1936	Ice Hockey
Kingsbury, Clarence	1908	Cycling, 20km
	1908	Cycling, Team Pursuit
Kinnear, William	1912	Rowing, Single Sculls
Kirby, Alister	1912	Rowing, Coxed Eights
Kirkwood, Jimmy	1988	Field Hockey
Knight, Arthur	1912	Football
Knowles, Durward[3]	1964	Sailing, Star Class
Knox, Debbie	2002	Curling

Lambert Chambers, Dorothea	1908	Lawn Tennis, Women's Singles
Lance, Thomas	1920	Cycling, Tandem
Lander, John	1928	Rowing, Coxless Fours
Larner, George	1908	Athletics, 3,500m Walk
	1908	Athletics, 10 Mile Walk
Laurie, Ran	1948	Rowing, Coxless Pairs
Law, Leslie	2004	Equestrian, 3-Day Event
Laws, Gilbert	1908	Sailing, 6m Class
Leaf, Charles	1936	Sailing, 6m Class
Leahy, Cornelius	1906[4]	Athletics, High Jump
Leighton, Arthur	1920	Field Hockey
Leman, Richard	1988	Field Hockey
Lessimore, Edward	1912	Shooting, 50m Small-bore Rifle Team
Lewis, Denise	2000	Athletics, Heptathlon
Lewis-Francis, Mark	2004	Athletics, 4x100m Relay
Liddell, Eric	1924	Athletics, 400m
Lindberg, Viktor	1900	Water Polo
Lindsay, Andrew	2000	Rowing, Coxed Eights
Lindsay, Robert	1920	Athletics, 4x400m Relay
Lister, William	1900	Water Polo
Littlewort, Henry	1912	Football
Llewellyn, Sir Harry	1952	Equestrian, Show Jumping Team
Lockett, Vivian	1920	Polo
Logan, Gerald	1908	Field Hockey
Longstaff, Tom	1924	Alpine & Mixed Alpinism (Reaching summit of Mt Everest 1922)
Lonsbrough, Anita	1960	Swimming, 200m Breaststroke
Lowe, Douglas	1920	Athletics, 800m
	1928	Athletics, 800m
MacBryan, Jack	1920	Field Hockey
MacDonald, Fiona	2002	Curling
MacDonald-Smith, Iain	1968	Sailing, Flying Dutchman Class
Macintosh, Henry	1912	Athletics, 4x100m Relay

Mackenzie, John	1908	Sailing, 12m Class
Mackinnon, Duncan	1908	Rowing, Coxless Fours
Mackworth-Praed, Cyril	1924	Shooting, Team Running Deer Double
Maclagan, Gilchrist	1908	Rowing, Coxed Eights
Maddison, William	1920	Sailing, 7m Class
Mallin, Harry	1924	Boxing, Middleweight
Mallory, George	1924	Alpine & Mixed Alpinism (Reaching summit of Mt Everest 1922)
Manning, Paul	2008	Cycling, Team Pursuit
Marcon, Charles	1920	Field Hockey
Martin, Albert	1908	Sailing, 12m Class
Martin, Leonard	1936	Yachting, 6m Class
Martin, Rhona	2002	Curling
Martin, Stephen	1988	Field Hockey
Matthews, Kenneth	1964	Athletics, 20km Walk
Matthews, Maurice	1908	Shooting, Small-bore Rifle Team
Matthews, Thomas (Johnnie)[2]	1906[4]	Cycling, 2,000m Tandem
Maudsley, Algernon[2]	1900	Sailing, ½-1 Ton Class
	1900	Sailing, Open Class
Maunder, Alexander	1908	Shooting, Team Trap
McBryan, John	1920	Field Hockey
McGrath, George	1920	Field Hockey
McIntyre, Michael	1988	Sailing, Star Class
McKane, Kathleen **see** Kitty Godfree		
McMeekin, Thomas	1908	Sailing, 6m Class
McNabb, James	1924	Rowing, Coxless Fours
McNair, Winifred	1920	Lawn Tennis, Women's Doubles
McTaggart, Dick	1952	Boxing, Lightweight
McWhirter, Douglas	1912	Football
Meade, Richard	1968	Equestrian, 3-Day Team
	1972	Equestrian, 3-Day Individual
	1972	Equestrian, 3-Day Team
Melvill, Teignmouth	1920	Polo
Meredith, Leonard 'Leon'	1908	Cycling, Team Pursuit
Merlin, Gerald	1906[4]	Shooting, Men's Trap, Single Shot 16m

Merlin, Sidney	1906[4]	Shooting, Men's Trap, Double Shot 14m
Merriman, Frederick	1908	Tug-of-War
Miller, Charles	1908	Polo
Miller, George	1908	Polo
Millner, Joshua	1908	Shooting, 100yds Free Rifle
Mills, Edwin	1908	Tug-of-War
	1920	Tug-of-War
Mitchell, Harry	1924	Boxing, Light Heavyweight
Moore, Belle	1912	Swimming, 4×100m Freestyle
Moore, Frank	1908	Shooting, Team Trap
Moore, Isabella	1912	Swimming, 4×100m Freestyle
Moorhouse, Adrian	1988	Swimming, 100m Breaststroke
Morris, John	1924	Alpine & Mixed Alpinism (Reaching summit of Mt Everest 1922)
Morris, Stewart	1948	Sailing, Swallow Class
Morrison, Robert	1924	Rowing, Coxless Fours
Morshead, Henry	1924	Alpine & Mixed Alpinism (Reaching summit of Mt Everest 1922)
Morton, Lucy	1924	Swimming, 200m Breaststroke
Morton, Margaret	2002	Curling
Murray, Robert	1912	Shooting, 50m Small-bore Rifle Team
Murray, Tom	1924	Curling
Nash, Tony	1964	Bobsleigh, Two-man
Neame, Philip	1924	Shooting, Team Running Deer Double
Nevinson, George	1908	Water Polo
Newall, Queenie	1908	Archery
Nicholas, J.	1900	Football
Nicholson, William	1928	Art, Graphic Works
Nickalls, Guy	1908	Rowing, Coxed Eights
Nickalls, Patteson	1908	Polo
Nightingale, Danny	1976	Modern Pentathlon
Noble, Alan	1908	Field Hockey

Noel, Evan	1908	Rackets, Men's Singles
Noel, John	1924	Alpine & Mixed Alpinism (Reaching summit of Mt Everest 1922)
Norton, Edward	1924	Alpine & Mixed Alpinism (Reaching summit of Mt Everest 1922)
O'Connor, Peter	1906[4]	Athletics, Hop, Step & Jump
O'Kelly, Con	1908	Wrestling, Heavyweight Freestyle
Ohuruogu, Christine	2008	Athletics, 400m
Oldman, Albert	1908	Boxing, Heavyweight
Osborn, John	1976	Sailing, Tornado Class
Ovett, Steve	1980	Athletics, 800m
Packer, Ann	1964	Athletics, 800m
Page, Edgar	1908	Field Hockey
Palmer, Charles	1908	Shooting, Team Trap
Pappin, Veryan	1988	Field Hockey
Parisi, Angelo[5]	1980	Judo, Heavyweight
Parker, Adrian	1976	Modern Pentathlon
Parker, Bridget	1972	Equestrian, 3-Day Team
Pattisson, Rodney	1968	Sailing, Flying Dutchman Class
	1972	Sailing, Flying Dutchman Class
Payne, Ernest	1908	Cycling, Team Pursuit
Peacock, William	1920	Water Polo
Pendleton, Victoria	2008	Cycling, Sprint
Pennell, Vane	1908	Rackets, Men's Doubles
Pepe, Joseph	1912	Shooting, 50m Small-bore Rifle Team
Percy, Iain	2000	Sailing, Finn Class
	2008	Sailing, Star Class
Perry, Herbert	1924	Shooting, Team Running Deer Double
Peters, Mary	1972	Modern Pentathlon
Pett, Billy	1906[4]	Cycling, 20 km

Phillips, Captain Mark	1972	Equestrian, 3-Day Team
Pike, James	1908	Shooting, Team Trap
Pimm, William	1908	Shooting, 50m Small Bore Rifle Team
Pinsent, Matthew	1992	Rowing, Coxless Pairs
	1996	Rowing, Coxless Pairs
	2000	Rowing, Coxless Fours
	2004	Rowing, Coxless Fours
Postans, John	1908	Shooting, Team Trap
Potter, Jon	1988	Field Hockey
Powlesland, Alfred	1900	Cricket
Pridmore, Reggie	1908	Field Hockey
Purcell, Noel	1920	Water Polo
Purchase, Zac	2008	Rowing, Lightweight Double Sculls
Purnell, Clyde	1908	Football
Quash, William	1900	Football
Queally, Jason	2000	Cycling, 1km Time Trial
Quentin, Cecil	1900	Sailing, 20+Ton Class
Radmilovic, Paulo	1908	Swimming, 4x200m Freestyle Relay
	1908	Water Polo
	1912	Water Polo
	1920	Water Polo
Rampling, Godfrey	1936	Athletics, 4x400m Relay
Rand, Mary	1964	Athletics, Long Jump
Rankin, Janice	2002	Curling
Rawlinson, Sir Alfred, 3rd Baronet	1900	Polo
Rawson, Ronald	1920	Boxing, Heavyweight
Redgrave, Sir Steven	1984	Rowing, Coxed Fours
	1988	Rowing, Coxless Pairs
	1992	Rowing, Coxless Pairs
	1996	Rowing, Coxless Pairs
	2000	Rowing, Coxless Fours

Redwood, Bernard	1908	Motor Boats, Class B
	1908	Motor Boats, Class C
Reed, Peter	2008	Rowing, Coxless Fours
Rees, Percy	1908	Field Hockey
Rhodes, John	1908	Sailing, 8m Class
Rimmer, John	1900	Athletics, 400m Steeplechase
	1900	Athletics, 5,000m Team
Ritchie, Josiah	1908	Lawn Tennis, Men's Singles
Rivett-Carnac, Charles	1908	Sailing, 7m Class
Rivett-Carnac, Frances	1908	Sailing, 7m Class
Roberts, William	1936	Athletics, 4x400m Relay
Robertson, Arthur 'Archie'	1908	Athletics, 3-Mile Team
Robertson, Arthur G	1900	Water Polo
Robertson, Shirley	2000	Sailing, Europe Class
	2004	Sailing, Yngling Class
Robinson, Eric	1900	Water Polo
Robinson, John	1908	Field Hockey
Robinson, Sidney	1900	Athletics, 5,000m Team
Romero, Rebecca	2008	Cycling, Individual Pursuit
Rook, Laurence	1956	Equestrian, 3-Day Team
Rushen, Arthur	1906[4]	Cycling, 2,000m Tandem
Russell, Arthur	1908	Athletics, 3,200m Steeplechase
Ryan, Harry	1920	Cycling, Tandem
Sanders, Terence	1924	Rowing, Coxless Fours
Sanderson, Ronald	1908	Rowing, Coxed Eights
Sanderson, Tessa	1984	Athletics, Javelin
Scarlett, Fred	2000	Rowing, Coxed Eights
Searle, Greg	1992	Rowing, Coxed Pairs
Searle, Jonny	1992	Rowing, Coxed Pairs
Sewell, John	1920	Tug-of-War
Sharpe, Ivan	1912	Football
Sheen, Gillian	1956	Fencing, Foil

Shepherd, John	1908	Tug-of-War
	1920	Tug-of-War
Sherwani, Imran	1988	Field Hockey
Shoveller, Stanley	1908	Field Hockey
	1920	Field Hockey
Simpson, Andrew	2008	Sailing, Star Class
Smith, Charles Sydney	1908	Water Polo
	1912	Water Polo
	1920	Water Polo
Smith, Herbert	1908	Football
Smith, William	1920	Field Hockey
Somers-Smith, John	1908	Rowing, Coxless Fours
Somervell, Howard	1924	Alpine & Mixed Alpinism (Reaching summit of Mt Everest 1922)
Southwood, Dick	1936	Rowing, Double Sculls
Spackman, F.G.	1900	Football
Speirs, Annie	1912	Swimming, 4x100m Freestyle
Spinks, Terry	1956	Boxing, Flyweight
Staff, Jamie	2008	Cycling, Team Sprint
Stamper, Harold	1912	Football
Stapleton, F.	1900	Water Polo
Stapley, Harold	1908	Football
Steer, Irene	1912	Swimming, 4x100m Freestyle
Stewart, Douglas	1952	Equestrian, Show Jumping Team
Stiff, Harry	1920	Tug-of-War
Stinchcombe, Archibald	1936	Ice Hockey
Strutt, Bill	1924	Alpine & Mixed Alpinism (Reaching summit of Mt Everest 1922)
Styles, William	1908	Shooting, Small Bore Rifle Disappearing Target
Sutton, Henry	1908	Sailing, 8m Class
Swann, Sidney	1912	Rowing, Coxed Eights
Syers, Madge	1908	Figure Skating
Symes, John	1900	Cricket
Tait, Gerald	1908	Sailing, 12m Class

Taylor, Henry	1908	Swimming, 400m Freestyle
	1908	Swimming, 1,500m Freestyle
	1908	Swimming, 4x200m Freestyle Relay
Taylor, Ian	1988	Field Hockey
Taylor, J. Howard	1900	Sailing, 3-10 Ton Class
Thomas, Geraint	2008	Cycling, Team Pursuit
Thomas, Henry	1908	Boxing, Bantamweight
Thompson, Alfred	1948	Art, Painting
Thompson, Daley	1980	Athletics, Decathlon
	1984	Athletics, Decathlon
Thompson, Don	1960	Athletics, 50km Walk
Thompson, Gordon	1908	Rowing, Coxless Pairs
Thorne, Ernest	1920	Tug-of-War
Thornycroft, Isaac	1908	Motor Boats, Class B
	1908	Motor Boats, Class C
Thould, Thomas	1908	Water Polo
Toller, Montague	1900	Cricket
Torvill, Jayne	1984	Ice Dancing
Trapmore, Steve	2000	Rowing, Coxed Eights
Triggs-Hodge, Andrew	2008	Rowing, Coxless Fours
Turnbull, Oswald (Noel)	1920	Lawn Tennis, Men's Doubles
Turner, R.R.	1900	Football
Tysoe, Alfred	1900	Athletics, 800m
	1900	Athletics, 5,000m Team
Vaile, Bryn	1988	Sailing, Star Class
Voigt, Emil	1908	Athletics, 5 Miles
Wakefield, Arthur	1924	Alpine & Mixed Alpinism (Reaching summit of Mt Everest 1922)
Walden, Harold	1912	Football
Warriner, Michael	1928	Rowing, Coxless Fours

Webb, Sarah	2004	Sailing, Yngling Class
	2008	Sailing, Yngling Class
Weldon, Frank	1956	Equestrian, 3-Day Team
Wells, Allan	1980	Athletics, 100m
Wells, Henry	1912	Rowing, Coxed Eights
West, Kieran	2000	Rowing, Coxed Eights
White, Reg	1976	Sailing, Tornado Class
White, Wilf	1952	Equestrian, Show Jumping Team
Whitlock, Harold	1936	Athletics, 50km Walk
Whitty, Allen	1924	Shooting, Team Running Deer Double
Wiggins, Bradley	2004	Cycling, Individual Pursuit
	2008	Cycling, Individual Pursuit
	2008	Cycling, Team Pursuit
Wilkie, David	1976	Swimming, 200m Breaststroke
Wilkinson, Cyril	1920	Field Hockey
Wilkinson, George	1900	Water Polo
	1912	Water Polo
Williams, Amy	2010	Skeleton
Williams, Steve	2004	Rowing, Coxless Fours
	2008	Rowing, Coxless Fours
Wilson, Herbert Haydon	1908	Polo
Wilson, Jack	1948	Rowing, Coxless Pairs
Wilson, Pippa	2008	Sailing, Yngling Class
Wodehouse, John (3rd Earl of Kimberley)	1920	Polo
Wolff, Frederick	1936	Athletics, 4x400m Relay
Wood, Arthur	1908	Sailing, 8m Class
Wood, Harvey	1908	Field Hockey
Woodward, Vivian	1908	Football
	1912	Football
Woosnam, Max	1920	Lawn Tennis, Men's Doubles
Wormwald, Leslie	1912	Rowing, Coxed Eights
Wright, Cyril	1920	Sailing, 7m Class
Wright, Dorothy	1920	Sailing, 7m Class

Wright, Gordon	1912	Football
Wyman, Robert	1936	Ice Hockey
Zealley, James	1900	Football

[1] Listed by the IOC but not by Mallon
[2] Listed by Mallon but not by the IOC
[3] Competing for the Bahamas
[4] The Second International Olympic Games (or 'Intercalated Games'), first included and subsequently excluded from Olympic records
[5] Won bronze medal in 1972 competing for Great Britain and, although his gold and two silver medals were won competing for France, IOC still have him as a British gold medallist

Bibliography

ARLOTT, John, ed., *The Oxford Companion to Sports and Games,* OUP, 1975.

BUCHANAN, Ian, 'Britain's First Olympic Champion: Launceston Elliot', in *Citius, Altius, Fortius,* (later *Journal of Olympic History*), Vol. 3, No.1 Winter 1997.

———, *British Olympians*, Guinness Publishing Ltd, London, 1999.

BUTCHER, Pat, *The Perfect Distance: Ovett and Coe: The Record-Breaking Rivalry,* Weidenfeld & Nicolson, London, 2004.

COLLINS, Mick, *All-Round Genius*, Aurum Press Ltd, London, 2006.

CAUGHEY, Ellen, *Eric Liddell: Olympian and Missionary,* Barbour Books, Uhrichsville OH, 2000.

FINNEGAN, Chris, *Self-portrait of a Fighting Man*, Macdonald and Jane's, London, 1976.

GILKEY, Langdon, *Shantung Compound,* Harper & Row, London, 1966.

GREEN, Geoffrey, *Kitty Godfree: Lady of a Golden Age*, Kingswood Press, London, 1987.

Huddersfield Daily Examiner, Interview December 13, 2003, Tony Pogson.

International Swimming Hall of Fame.

KENT, Graeme, *Olympic Follies*, JR Books, London, 2008.

KITTERMASTER, Charlotte, 'The Beijing Olympic Games: an analysis of the human rights issues', LLM dissertation, Birkbeck, University of London, 2008,

LENNARTZ, Karl, 'The 2nd International Olympic Games in Athens 1906' in *Journal of Olympic History,* Vol 10 ISOH, December 2001/January 2002.

MCCANN, Liam, *The Olympics: Facts, Figures and Fun*, Sterling Publishing Co. Inc., 2006

MILLER, David, *The Official History of the Olympic Games and the IOC: Athens to Beijing, 1894-2008*, Mainstream Publishing Co., Edinburgh, 2008.

NELSON, Cordner & QUERCETANI, Roberto, *The Milers*, Tafnews Press, California, 1985.

Observer Sport Monthly, Sunday 5 March, 2006.

PINSENT, Matthew, *A Lifetime in a Race,* Ebury Press, London, 2004.

RIDDOCH, Andrew & KEMP, John, *When the Whistle Blows: The Story of the Footballers' Battalion in the Great War*, J H Haynes & Co Ltd, London, 2008.

SEARS, Edward, 'The Revival of the Olympic Games' in *Running through the Ages*, McFarland, 2001.

SMITH, P. R., *Great Moments of Sportsmanship*, privately published, London, 2008.

Sport: the interactive issue, May 2012.

VOIGT, Robin, 'Emil Voigt, the Unique Olympian' in *Journal of Olympic History*, Vol 16, ISOH, December 2008.

WALLECHINSKY, David & LOUKEY, Jaime, *The Complete Book of the Olympics*, Aurum Press, London, 2008.

WIGGINS, Bradley, *In Pursuit of Glory*, Orion Books Ltd, London, 2008

YAPP, Nick, *Chasing Gold: Centenary of the British Olympic Association*, British Olympic Association (with Getty Images), 2005.

websites:

www.azhockey.com

www.bbc.co.uk/Manchester

www.bbc.co.uk/sport/0/olympics/2012

www.belfasttelegraph.co.uk

www.britishrowing.org.uk

www.brunel.ac.uk

www.dailymail.co.uk/sport/olympics

www.ericliddell.org

www.guardian.co.uk/Sport

www.history1900s.about.com

www.independent.co.uk

www.inthewinningzone.com

www.isoh.org

www.la84foundation.org

www.london2012.com

www.news.bbc.co.uk

www.olympic.org

olympics.sporting99.com

www.sailing.org/olympics

www.sportscorrespondent.info

www.sports-reference.com

www.telegraph.co.uk

www./terrifictop10.wordpress.com/category/sports-leisure

www.thenorthernecho.co.uk

www.thisislondon.co.uk

www.timesonline.co.uk

www.trackandfield.about.com/od/polevault

www.wikipedia.com

Index of People

List of Abbreviations

AAA   Amateur Athletic Association (now Amateur Athletic Association of England)
ADC   Aide-de-Camp
ASA   Amateur Swimming Association
BBC   British Broadcasting Corporation
BOA   British Olympic Association
BSJA   British Show Jumping Association
CBE   Companion (of the Most Excellent Order) of the British Empire
DBE   Dame Commander (of the Most Excellent Order) of the British Empire
DSO   Distinguished Service Order
FC   Football Club
FINA   Fédération Internationale de Natation
GHS   George Herbert Stancer (event)
IAAF   International Association of Athletics Federations OR International Amateur Athletic Federation
IABF   International Amateur Boxing Federation
IOC   International Olympic Committee
ISAF   International Sailing Federation
ISOH   International Society of Olympic Historians
ISU   International Skating Union
KBE   Knight Commander (of the Most Excellent Order) of the British Empire
LOCOG London Organising Committee of the Olympic and Paralympic Games
MBE   Member (of the Most Excellent Order) of the British Empire
MCC   Marylebone Cricket Club
OBE   Officer (of the Most Excellent Order) of the British Empire
OPEN   Olympic and Paralympic Employment Network
TT   Time Trial
UCI   Union Cycliste Internationale

Also from Medina Publishing Ltd

GREENWICH AND THE LONDON RIVER
Paul Tempest
illustrations by Peter Kent; photographs by Stephen Tempest
170 x 240 mm, Portrait
208 pp Softback with gatefold
ISBN: 978-09567801-9-9
Price £9.95

Publication: 19 May 2012

THE ARAB HORSE
Peter Upton
285 x 234 mm, landscape
344 pp, casebound
ISBN: 978-0-9570234-0-6
(Medina Publishing Ltd in association with Arabian Horse World AG)
Price £45
Publication: 15 May 2012

ROYAL HERITAGE The Story of Jordan's Arab Horses
HRH Princess Alia al Hussein & Peter Upton
210 x 218 mm Portrait
264 pp Hardback
ISBN: 978-0-9564170-4-6
Price: £35
Illustrated throughout with paintings, drawings,
sketches and historical photographs

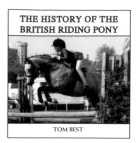

THE HISTORY OF THE BRITISH RIDING PONY
Tom Best
210 x 218 mm Portrait
300 pp Hardback
ISBN: 978-0-9564170-9-1
Price £35
Illustrated throughout with historical and contemporary photographs

KALILA AND DIMNA Fables of Conflict and Intrigue
Ramsay Wood
Illustrations by G M Whitworth: Foreword by Michael Wood
200 x 148 mm Portrait
224 pp Softbound
ISBN: 978-0-9567081-0-6
Price £9.95
Publication: January 2012
Illustrated throughout with line drawings

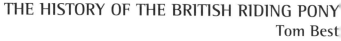

Medina Publishing

info@medinapublishing.com   www.medinapublishing.com

Registered office
Medina Publishing Ltd
9 St John's Place
Newport
Isle of Wight PO30 1LH

Correspondence
83 Ewell Road
Surbiton
Surrey KT6 6AH
Telephone: +44 (0)208 3997736

Distribution
Central Books
99 Wallis Road
London E9 5LN
orders@centralbooks.com